Thayer, Thomas N.
    The Yellowstone River Country of Montana
    and Wyoming © 1996
    Bibliography: p. 114
    Includes Index.
Copyright Control # 70-533-0047(T)
LC - 96-250089
ISBN -
    Hardcover - 0-9652439-0-7
    Softcover - 0-9652439-1-5

The Eagle
By Hall Diteman

THE EAGLE FLEW...
AND
FOUND THE
YELLOWSTONE
COUNTRY

This is a country stretching from the Gallatin Mountains in the west, south to Wyoming's Wind River Mountains, most of the Absaroka Beartooths, north to the Bridgers, and taking water from the Crazys, then gathering in the drainages of the Pryors, Big Horns, and Wolf Mountains and all of the prairies and scab hills from Big Timber to the Missouri in North Dakota.

This is an area in square miles larger than New England and bigger than most states and some of the world's most spectacular creations in natural sculptured landscapes.

The mountains create, influence, and give the rivers energy.

If worship were of the sun, the moon, the snow, the mountains and the Yellowstone River, there would be many Sundays in thought flying over this view.

The Yellowstone River Country is ruled by these three, grumpy, old men.

TABLE OF CONTENTS

Yellowstone River Country Montana-Wyoming

1. **Introduction**

2. **Mountain Region**

3. **Big Horn Basin**

4. **Powder River Basin**

5. **Yellowstone Park Region**

6. **Middle Yellowstone Region**

7. **Lower Yellowstone Region**

8. **Conclusion**

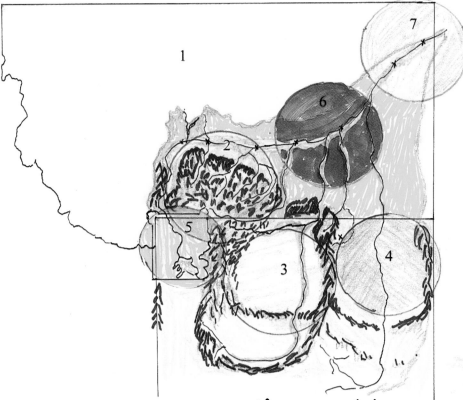

The following pages are an enticement to visit the mountains, rivers and prairies.

Preface by Conrad Burns

Dear Friends:

WELCOME TO THE LAND OF THE BIG SKY... WELCOME TO OUR LIVING ROOM....   IT IS JUST A PART OF GOD'S MAGNIFICENT CREATION...

You are in for a real treat as you immerse yourself into the history and lore of this magnificent part of our planet. No land offers more of the mystique of the West and the Big Sky Country than here in this book.

After you have used this book as a guide for your travels here, it will keep your memories of this special place alive for years to come.

Here is the history of ranching, energy production, timbering, and mining and how the men and women of the land learned to manage the natural resources and protect the land for a true quality of life for man and wildlife.

Tom's great work is for your enjoyment and that you might get a little more insight about this fragile country. It is truly accurate. Enjoy....

INTRODUCTION

- Area maps

- Areas

- Overview of the Yellowstone River Country

- Montana's Yellowstone Country

- Yellowstone River

- Early men to visit the country

- Early American Indians

Wintertime on the Yellowstone River

Montana and Wyoming's Yellowstone Country

Introduction

Time never stands and the natural illustration of change is everywhere. These are views of regions in which change came, went, came again, and left beauty, austere terrain, and wealth, as if planned.

The general look is an overview from hints of earliest time until now and even though the segments are interwoven, they are distinct. These segments encompass time and result as if written yesterday.

Whether the mountains came before the rivers or both happened in the same era is not as important as today's scene.

Unfolding is a look at the creation, allowing life to enjoy living in these spectacular settings, to participate in its care, to share its wealth, and to leave for our children.

The valley residents need to understand their surroundings: the history, the geology, the geography, and the effectual living with all.

Often, as individuals, we separate and look askance at the happenings around us; saying empathetically, the action is out of my control while only one voice or one action may be enough to turn events.

We must use, but we must care and share. There is no such eventuality as one for all and all for one. The planet around us can heal from abuse, but why make this the priority.

This is a look at an intermingled history which hopefully allows us to see how close we are to the rocks, the sky, the water, and our surroundings.

And, if we drive an automobile, how dependent upon extraction we have become. If we drink a soda, how dependent we have become on the

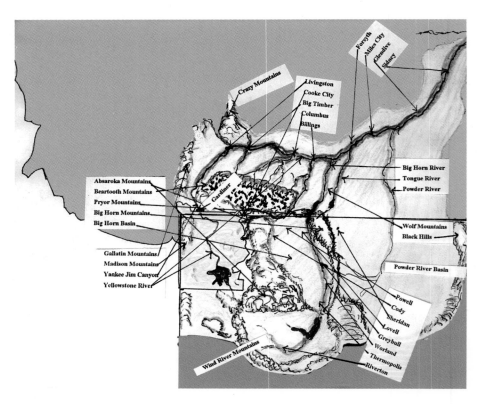

sugar grown from the water, and if we eat the beef, how close we are to the rough land growing the grass.

We can and must entwine with each other and, hopefully, this collage will entice to __understand, the understanding__ of living together.

The Lewis and Clark Expedition named the Yellowstone River after the yellow standstone bluffs where the river carved its valley from Livingston, Montana to the Missouri River.

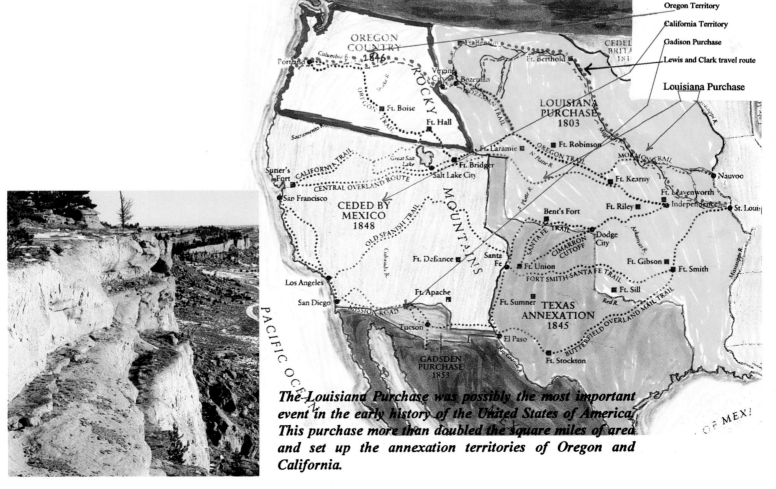

The Louisiana Purchase was possibly the most important event in the early history of the United States of America. This purchase more than doubled the square miles of area and set up the annexation territories of Oregon and California.

Montana's Yellowstone Country

The Yellowstone River

The south wilderness area of the *Yellowstone Park* is as remote as any area in the continental United States. Here is the beginning of the *Yellowstone River* off the slopes of the Mount Yountz to have its waters to travel about 70 miles to *Yellowstone Lake*. Water, pure, cold, and clean from this very remote section of mountains is much the same as if we could turn the clock back 200 years.

The water gathers in *Yellowstone Lake* to flow out of the north end beginning a journey to the *Gulf of Mexico*.

What is so special is the total mass of wilderness protecting the environment of the upper river drainage before man, agriculture, industry, and towns can tamper with this pristine fluid. The *Yellowstone River* makes a three-quarter circle out of the park to Livingston, Montana, east to Billings, Miles City, Glendive, then north to Sidney and finally to the Missouri at Williston, North Dakota, 670 dam-free miles from beginning to end. The trip through Montana gives life to farms, ranches, small towns, tourism, Billings and other cities along the way.

Yellowstone Lake is part of the old caldera of former volcanic eruptions creating the *Yellowstone National Park*. The mud pots, geysers, mineral hot springs are a reminder of how close molten hot lavas are to the surface in this area.

The upper river from the lake to upper falls, lower falls, *Yellowstone's Grand Canyon* mixes along the way with mineral rich hot springs creating the world famous trout stream. Trout thrive in this mineral rich, cold, and high oxygenated water. The management of the fishery is catch and release so trout have the opportunity to grow, spawn, and keep their numbers despite the heaviest fishing pressure per mile of streams in America.

The river collects water along the way from the *Absaroka* and *Beartooth Mountains* then in one final outburst the river flows out of the park at Gardiner, Montana into *Yankee Jim Canyon*. Here in the rough, rocky canyon, the river narrows and deepens flowing around big rocks. This haven harbors some world record brown trout weighing over 20 pounds, a true fisherman's paradise.

The river out of *Yankee Jim Canyon* now contends with irrigation, roadways, railroad tracks, and floating boat fisherman. The river turns east at *Livingston* leaving the granites and volcanic formations of the mountains behind

to flow past the yellow sedimentary rimrocks as the valley widens on its way to the *Missouri*.

Looking at the *Yellowstone Valley* from Livingston down river, imagine how the waters from melting glaciers of several thousand years ago sent volumes of silt, mud, gravel, and boulders to carve this valley, now fertile and unique, through the temperate Montana desert. The water irrigates cropland growing alfalfa hay, barley, wheat, corn, sugar beets, and cattle all contributing to the *two billion dollars of Montana annual agricultural income*. Towns and cities along its way use the water for lawns, parks, golf courses, and other domestic and industrial needs.

The Beartooths, Absarokas, Bridgers, Crazys, Pryors, and Big Horn Mountains all add water flow to the Yellowstone River sending an average 9,476,000-acre feet of liquid to the Gulf of Mexico annually.

The expedition of *Lewis and Clark* passed the mouth of the *Yellowstone River* in the early spring of 1805. On the way back to St. Louis, *Captain William Clark* traveled down the Yellowstone River and about 25 miles east of now Billings, Montana carved his name in the famous *Pompey's Pillar on Friday, July 25, 1806*. The French and Indians called the river Elk River but the expedition gave the name Yellowstone after the yellow sandstone bluffs along each side of the valley.

The Yellowstone River

Yankee Jim Canyon

Here is where the Yellowstone River forced its way through granite, upthrust rock.

Deep in these blue pools are record, brown trout difficult to catch.

Cottonwood of Age
by Charles Fritz

The river shares many faces as it flows from high mountains to the Missouri River. Soft autumn colors of reds and yellows and the browns of the rimrocks stretch for miles along the river's path.

Pompey's Pillar is a sandstone rock caricature of a Roman pillar carved by the Yellowstone River where Captain William Clark stopped while traveling downstream to the Missouri River in 1806. Scratched in the sandstone is: "Captain William Clark, July 25, 1806

From the Lewis and Clark Journals

Thursday April 25th 1805

the water friezed on the oars this morning as the men rowed. about 10 oclock A.M. the wind began to blow so violently that we were obliged to lye low. my dog had been absent during the last night, and I was fearful we had lost him altogether, however, much to my satisfaction he joined us at 8 oclock this morning. Knowing that the river was crooked, from the report of the hunters who were out yesterday, and beleiving that we were at no very great distance from the Yellow stone River; I determined, in order as mush as possible to avoid detention, to proceed by land with a few men to the entrance of that river and make the necessary observations to determine its position; accordingly I set out at 11 OCk. on the Lard. side, accompanyed by four men. when we had proceeded about four miles, I ascended the hills from whence I had a most pleasing view of the country, particularly of the wide and fertile vallies formed by the missouri and the yellowstone rivers, which occasionally unmasked by the wood on their borders disclose their meanderings for many miles in their passage through these delightfull tracts of country. I determined to encamp on the banks of the Yellow stone river which made it's appearance about 2 miles South of me. the whol face of the country was covered with herds of Buffaloe, Elk & Antelopes; deer are also abundant, but keep themselves more concealed in the woodland. the buffaloe Elk and Antelope are so gentle that we pass near them while feeding, without appearing to excite any alarm among them; and when we attract their attention, they frequently approach us more nearly to discover what we are, and in some instances pursue us a consideration distance apparently with that view. we encamped on the bank of the yellow stone river, 2 miles South of it's confluence with the Missouri.

Monday, June 30th 1806

...Clark will take the rest of the party to the forks of the Beaverhead, where the boats were left last fall. After the boats have been put in condition, he will select a detachment to take them to the Great Falls and help those whom Lewis has left there portage the whole outfit round the falls. (These two detachments will then descend the Missouri by boat to the general rendezvous, the mouth of the Yellowstone, picking up Lewis and his small party at the mouth of the Marias.) Clark will take the others overland to the Yellowstone and down it to some point where it appears to become navigable. From that point he will send Sergeant Pryor with the horses to the mouth of the Yellowstone. After making dugouts, he and the others will take them down the Yellowstone to its mouth.

First Montana Settlement

After the expedition Manuel Lisa organized the Lisa, Menard, Morrison, and Company, the first of the American fur trappers. They engaged George Droullard, hunter and interpreter for Lewis & Clark and John Colter, to go back into the Rocky Mountains with them in 1807.

During this trip John Colter made his famous five-hundred mile circle from Fort Manuel Lisa (first permanent settlement in Montana) at the mouth of the Big Horn River into Yellowstone Park. Colter found the land of many smokes but everybody called him the great liar of the west.

After several successful years trapping, in the fall of 1808, John Colter and James Potts trapped the Jefferson River together. They were jumped by the Blackfeet and captured. Potts was killed immediately. Colter was stripped naked and told to run for his life. Running naked through the rock and cactus he outdistanced all but one of the Indians which he killed with the brave's own spear. He ran to the Madison River and his under the water in a log drift. About seven days later with his feet full of cactus and nearly starved, he reached Fort Manuel Lisa about 250 miles downstream. A feat no one would try to repeat.

Routes Used Across the Rocky Mountain Area

The time periods of influence in the movement of Americans from the early 1800s into the Rocky Mountains can be traced to:

First, the search for a water route to the Pacific Ocean. This was the political decision after Thomas Jefferson's purchase of the Louisiana Territory from France.

Second, after the Lewis and Clark trek from St. Louis, Missouri to the Pacific coast, the lure of the mountains was to trap beaver for pelts to sell to the European hat market.

Third, this fur-trapping period lasted from 1807 to 1840 when the caravans of settlers embarked: to Oregon by way of the Oregon Trail, to California by way of the central overland route and by way of the Old Spanish Trail to southern California, and others such as the Santa Fe Trail.

Fourth, in this mix was gold, land, and buffalo meats and hides.

All that slowed this mass of movement was Indians. Many small, medium, and large tribes who had already staked claim to this country were resistant to the white settlers and gold miners.

The routes across Indian land created conflict after conflict as the Indian's life and lifestyle was threatened.

Early Dates of Note

1805 Lewis & Clark traveled through Montana

1807 John Colter traveled into the Yellowstone Country to open fur trade

1812 War of 1812 against the British

1822 Jim Bridger began trapping the mountains under General Ashley's command

1835 Jim led a major party into the mountains

1840 End of the fur trade

1854 Beginning of the Oregon Trail

1851 The United States setup a treaty with the Crow Indians recognizing the Absaroka Beartooth Mountains and the Yellowstone Valley as belonging to the Crow Nation.

1863 Bozeman Trail and discovery of gold in Montana

Civil War between the states

1872 The set aside of Yellowstone Park

1876 Custer's Last Stand/Battle of the Little Big Horn

1877 Nez Perce march

1877 General Miles winter battle with the Sioux

1882 The Crows ceded the Mountain areas of Beartooth/Absaroka to the United States government allowing this interior area to be under federal control setting up probably the first wilderness area.

1883 The railroad through Montana

1909 Homesteading in Montana, Wyoming, etc.

1910 Barbed wire

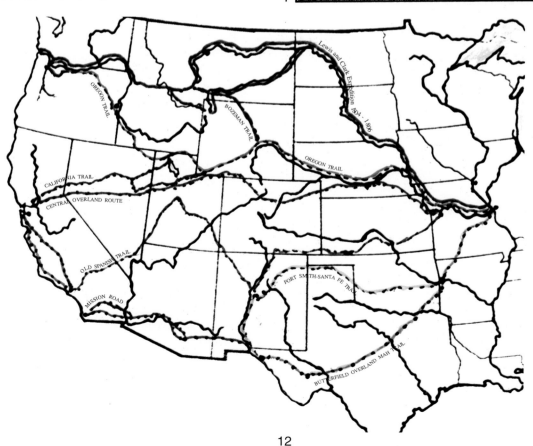

The early Paleo Indians seemed to have disappeared sometime after the recent glaciers.

The Clovis Indians hunting the biggest North American game, the mammoth elephant.

Early Paleo Indians lived in the Pryor Mountain caves.
Note the darkened areas from fires.

Steamboat Mountain pictograph

Early American Indians

The history of the American Indians is still a mystery to anthropologists but without trying to explain the migrations from Asia, points of interest can be gathered from the early *Paleo Indians*.

These Indians were hunters, fishermen, and gatherers during the time of the woolly mammoth and saber-toothed tigers.

They were small family groups living around lakes where they could fish, hunt birds, and larger game.

The point of interest evolving from the Paleo Indians to the modern Indians are the small family units probably extending into larger groups called tribes.

The Indians had trouble with large social groups. Their structure of government formed loose associations but not broad areas or numbers of tribes working together to accomplish a unified front.

Possible exceptions were the early Mound Indians or Central American Indians who seemed to live together in larger numbers but even then they were one tribe.

Looking at the North American Continent, the numbers of tribal groups illustrate how widely-spread the Indians were, and also how dissected they were in whatever might be termed togetherness or government.

These loose associations worked to their demise with the white Europeans who could generate government, cohesiveness, and common goals for their large numbers regardless of ethnic groups.

The next conclusion with regard to the dissection of Indians was the tribes remained hunters, gatherers, and travelers rather than large established city groups and the horse added to this independence.

The coastal tribes had a great bounty of fish, seal, walrus, elk, and caribou while the Central Plains Indian enjoyed buffalo, deer, antelope, and elk in abundance rivaling the African game herds.

The Indians were really tribal units occupying an area in which they had the ability to control. Fierce battles, raids, and wars were always present in their lives. Truly, the strongest survived and controlled the hunting areas.

This constant war was a lifestyle creating deep enemies among the groups. Thus, when they needed to unite and fight the white man, they could not overcome the mistrust among the tribes or Indian nations.

The modern Indians migrated from the east coast of America.

Indian Brave
By Rob McClellan
Courtesy of Taos Drums

Early American Indians

When Lewis and Clark came to the mouth of the Yellowstone River in 1805, the controlling tribes in Montana were the Crows claiming the middle Yellowstone country through to the Wind River Mountains and the east side of the Beartooth-Absaroka Mountain Range. The Cheyenne and Sioux were in the Dakotas and eastern Wyoming country.

The horse brought from Europe by the Spaniards helped the Plains Indians become the greatest hunters the world had known.

The Blackfeet coming down from Canada controlled the area of the Northern Rockies through the Madison River drainage, south to the west side of the Tetons of Idaho.

The Crows and the Blackfeet were enemies and an example of how the Indians could not cooperate. These tribes were always raiding each other's camps.

The Shoshone or Snake Indians of Central Wyoming and Jackson Hole were another strong group. They also used the headwaters of the Green River as their hunting grounds.

The west side of the Rocky Mountains were controlled by what was termed the Great Basin Indians: Bannack, Paiute, and Western Shoshone.

The plateau Indians: Nez Perce, Flatheads, Kalispell, Kootenai, etc. exerted some influence in the Rocky Mountain areas. Also many smaller groups were ebbing and flowing through the mountains.

Some groups such as the Crow, Sioux, Blackfeet, Cheyenne, Shoshone were hunting tribes traveling in and out of their areas following the game herds living in teepees and completely dependent on the horse.

Some tribes were friends of the white man and some dedicated enemies. Disease, especially smallpox, was disastrous to the Indian populations. Some tribes lost up to 80% of their numbers.

After the 1840s, disease, whisky, killing of the buffalo, and broken treaties are all part of the downfall of the Plains, Basin, and Plateau Indians covering what is now Montana, Wyoming, Idaho, and adjoining lands.

Men like Jim Bridger enjoyed excellent relationships with many groups of Indians, but the military, pioneers, homesteaders, and miners were constantly in conflict with the Native Americans.

While the Indians were savage in the killing of whites, the U. S. military brutalized women and children displaying little honor in these exploits. Neither side can find more blame than the other. When the Indians did succumb to the U. S. government treaties, subsequent presidents probably would not honor those agreements which had been written before him.

Tribal acquistion of the horse

15

In the 1840s 63 million buffalo roamed the areas west of the Mississippi River.

The coming of the white explorers, then the settlers, changed life forever for the early Indians...

The pressures of greed were the controlling factors in the U. S. government policy during these years.

Today's world of the American Indian is not too much better than at the turn of the century.

Reservations are both a problem and a blessing. They give the Indian a place, but also limit his ability to become adjusted to today's world. Today is today, yesterday is gone. The Indian must find self-sufficiency within this climate of economics. The reservations tend to restrict this adjustment.

Next to the horse and the buffalo, the beaver was most important to the western movement. Fur traders and trappers traveled into the Rocky Mountains coming back with great stories of wonder adding to the excitement of "go west young man."

The Meadowlark sings the prairie song

Hollow Horn Bear
Sioux Chief
By Paul Scheben

the Sarpy Creek Area earning royalties of two million dollars each year to the tribal council.

The reservation includes parts of the Big Horn River, Big Horn Mountains, Pryor Mountains, and a broad expanse of prairie land. *Selling recreation* could create major income dollars for the council in the future.

As is often the case, Chief Plenty Coups seemed a visionary which put him in the standing of Sitting Bull, Chief Joseph, and other tribal leaders of his time.

Until Lewis and Clark, only French-Canadian trappers had visited the Missouri River Country.

Chief Plenty Coups

The famous Crow chief born in 1848 carried on the affairs of the Crow Indians until his death in 1932. He donated land and his home for a museum on the Crow Indian Reservation in the town of Pryor, Montana. The museum houses his personal belongings as well as a history of the Crow Indians.

Chief Plenty Coups took the path of not warring with the whites. As a result, the United States government allowed two million acres for the Crow Indian Reservation.

This reservation is much larger than what was set aside for other Montana-Wyoming tribes and has coal reserves in

Chief Plenty Coups
Crow Indian Chief
By Leroy Greene
Courtesy of Ella Greene

One of the first Americans to travel into the Yellowstone, Beartooth, Absaroka Mountain areas was John Colter and...

As he walked out of the mountains down the Shoshone River he came to what was to be known as Colter's Hell.

COLTER'S HELL

John Colter, veteran of the Lewis and Clark Expedition, notably self-sufficient mountain man and indefatigable explorer, was the first white man known to have reconnoitered this locale. In 1807, possibly traveling alone but probably escorted by Crow guides, he crossed the Stinking Water (Shoshone River) via a major Indian-trail ford located about a mile downstream from this observation point. Here, extending along both sides of the river, he discovered an active geyser district. Steam mixed with sulfur fumes and shooting flames escaped through vents in the valley floor, subterranean rumblings were ominously audible. Although mineralized hot springs continue to flow along the river's edge, the eruptions Colter watched are now marked only by cones of parched stone.

This was primarily Shoshone and Crow country but other Indians came to the area. Particularly Bannocks and Nez Percé, journeying eastward over the mountains to hunt the plains buffalo, tarried to test the heralded medicinal values of these "stinking waters" baths. Ranged along bench-lands to the east and north are numerous tepee rings, evidence of former Indian encampments. Heart Mountain, famous landmark and geological oddity, is conspicuous on the northern horizon.

Honoring a respected predecessor, mountain men of the 1820's-1830's fur trade heyday named this place Colter's Hell. Later, early-day officials of Yellowstone Park applied that name to the Park's geyser area -- thereby causing a degree of historic confusion. The true Colter's Hell is here in view.

Colter's Hell Canyon west of Cody, Wyoming is much the same today as yesterday.

The canyon shows how flood waters leave scars exposing the history of mountain activity in and around Yellowstone Park.

The Lure of the Mountains

*After Colter's stories were told
in the east, mountain men like
Jim Bridger and Joe Meeks
filtered into the Rocky Mountains*

Jim Bridger, often called *Old Gabe* by the white mountain men and *Blanket Chief* by the Indians, was without doubt the great mountain man of the Yellowstone country.

Jim entered into the Rocky Mountain adventures as a fur trapper, Indian trader, explorer, and scout traveling with General Ashley in 1822. He was a boy of 16 years and until his death at 77, he had traversed the Rocky Mountain Yellowstone Country more than any man.

His ability to smell Indian trouble and escape served him well but even then some times were tough. Once in a scrimmage with the Blackfeet he ended near death with two arrows in his back. One of Bridger's fur trapper friends took his skinning knife and cut one arrow out but could not get the other, so he cut off the sinew and took the shaft.

Jim carried this arrow head for three years until the surgeon, Reverend Marcus Whitman, cut out the three-inch head. It had been hooked under a bone.

The stories are many and these old-timers were the best at exaggeration.

The Montana gold fever hit in 1863 and men with wagon trains wanted to use the Bozeman Trail via the Sioux hunting grounds to get to Bozeman. The early treaties at Fort Laramie gave the Sioux, Cheyenne, and Crows the area of the Big Horn Mountains, north to the Yellowstone, and out into Nebraska as their buffalo hunting grounds.

Stories flooded the men's imagination about gold and Jim Bridger would fan this curiosity with "out thar in the Yellowstone Country thar war a mountain with a great big diamond on it. Any man lucky enough to git the sun right could see it fur 50 miles." One man in the wagon train offered Jim a good rifle and his best horse for the right direction to the mountain.

Putting all the stories aside, the whites backed by the U. S. Government and the military were bound to travel the Bozeman Trail to Montana country. Jim was hired as scout by Colonel Carrington to venture to Sheridan, Wyoming country to build forts along the road for protection.

The bloody Sioux war cost many lives as the military and wagon trains took foolish risks without heed to Jim's advice. During this time the Indians Ogalala, Minnconjou, Hunkpapa, Cheyenne, Arapaho, and Gros Ventres using these hunting grounds were uniting to attack the forts before the snow flew.

Jim Bridger was sent out to survey a road and assess the Indian strength around the Big Horn Mountains. He counted many Indian lodges along the Tongue River. The rumor was they were readying to attack Fort Phil Kearney.

The Indians made a mockery of the inexperienced and outmanned military. Scrimmage after scrimmage was taking place mostly in favor of the Indians.

When Colonel Fetterman was sent to Fort Phil Kearney, he wished to show his courage and generalship. He bragged "with 80 men I could ride through the Sioux." Jim Bridger told the group they were crazy, but these soldiers from the Civil War knew everything and thought the Indians were no match.

On the morning of December 6, 1866, Colonel Fetterman and Lieutenant Bingham had their first encounter with the Sioux. The soldiers came back whipped and left their dead in the woods not far from the fort.

Several days later Fetterman and Grummond, in a hurry to whip the Sioux, took 78 officers and men out of the fort and two civilians with repeating Henry rifles to bring back the wood wagons. They were fooled into chasing some Indians into a trap. In less than forty minutes the Sioux had killed, mutilated, and scalped every man.

Finally, the U. S. government abandoned the Bozeman Trail and Fort Phil Kearney was soon burned by the Sioux.

After the fur trappers, men were sponsored by Congress to learn the truth about the Indians and the Rocky Mountains...

Famous Men

The people of the eastern United States had an unquenchable thirst to know about the mountains and the Indians of the West.

Some famous men of the mountains emerged besides trappers, cowboys, and Indian fighters.

Headwaters of the Green River
Thomas Moran
Courtesy of Buffalo Bill Historical Center

Ferdinand Hayden, Director of the U. S. Geological Survey, led a group to explore the Yellowstone park country in 1871. Taking his party of 34 men into the park area was significant because the expedition carried young painter, Thomas Moran, and photographer, William Henry Jackson.

The stories told by John Colter, Jim Bridger, and Joe Meek of the geysers, mud pots, and Yellowstone River Canyon were so compelling Congress appropriated $40,000 to settle the rumors and bring back evidence of these wonders.

The paintings and photographs were just what was needed to convince the American public to create Yellowstone Park in 1872. The five-hundred-page report backed with photographs and paintings left no doubt this was a premier natural area of the world.

Thomas Moran's painting are still considered some of the best illustrations of the park area.

George Catlin - 1832 Expedition

George began his business life as a lawyer but sometime during 1828 he wrote the secretary of war about traveling west to paint Indian activities. His urgency was to record their lifestyle before it vanished.

His dream was to become a "history painter." Even though the secretary's halls were covered with early paintings of eastern Indians, the United States government was reluctant to commission more Indian art.

In 1832 he began his tour from St. Louis to Fort Union, an 1,800 mile trip up the Missouri River without help from the government. His help came from the American Fur Company. During this tour he painted the Mandans of North Dakota, the Crows and Blackfeet of Montana, and in 1836 the Indians in the regions of the southwest, the Mississippi, and the Great Lakes.

George amassed some 607 paintings of Indians and their activities. During this time he appealed time and again to the government for help, for expenses, and for a gallery to exhibit his paintings.

Our young government was having money problems and southern congressmen did not see the need to spend money for Indian history.

Catlin, finding little support for his work in America, took his display to England and France and spent many years overseas. During this time he continued to try to have congress add the collection to the Smithsonian.

So, as the first visionary and showman trying to make a living from his art, he was rebuffed by his own country demonstrating again how immature our young government was during the 1800s.

Crow Chief
George Catlin
Courtesy of Buffalo Bill Historical Center

Mountain Regions

- Mountain Formation
- Earth Age Chart
- Volcanoes
- Yellowstone Park Formation
- Beartooth-Absaroka Mountains
- Pryor Mountains
- Big Horn Canyon
- Big Horn Mountains

Iron statue of Jim Bridger in the town of Bridger, Montana. Just a look away from the Beartooth Mountains. Jim Bridger in Indian country where "A sharp eye breeds a lot of good luck."

Indians on a Bluff Surveying General Miles' Troops
Charles Marion Russell
Courtesy of Buffalo Bill Historical Center

The mountain formation by compression and uplifting was a monster happening in the re-shaping of the Yellowstone Country...

The Rocky Mountains began their uplifting

The Mesozoic Age which included Triassic, Jurassic, and Cretaceous were the most important of the geological periods. During this time shallow seas covered the land from the Arctic Ocean to the Gulf of Mexico. Around these seas and swamps grew large forests where the dinosaurs gained dominance over the kingdom.

The Triassic Age began 245 million years ago and as this era evolved into the Jurassic Age, the reptiles, birds, trees, gastropods evolved and spread. The Cretaceous Era continued the many changes and evolution of these animals groups.

About the time between 70 million and 60 million years, the Pacific plate and the Continental plates began compression by moving toward each other. This compression initiated the uplifting of the Rocky Mountains, completely changing the climates of the region.

The climates now created by the mountains were wet forests on the west side, to dry deserts on the east side. Instead of swamps producing coal fields, grasslands began to dominate and extend from Montana-Wyoming country across to Nebraska and surrounding areas.

The dinosaurs became extinct, plant life was more varied, and numerous species of mammals occupied the region. The many species surviving were those capable of change and, during the Miocene epoch, horses, camels, rhinos, and elephants evolved.

The formation of mountains called the Laramide orogeny was basically complete during the Eocene epoch but the change continues through to the present time with volcanic activity, erosion, and glaciation.

Today, the Rocky Mountain complex of Absaroka-Beartooth, Wind Rivers, Pryors, Big Horns, and others, control or effect our weather from day to day and season to season.

Understanding the mountains and how they affect our lives is of great interest because the mountains give the Yellowstone country an enjoyable and varied climate.

Mountain Formation Faults, Stacking, and Volcanoes

Plate stacking Bridger Mountains

Pryor Mountain Fault

A mountain fault is a line where one face slips by another, sometimes under or over, or upward or downward. In any event, portions of the mountain block move and the fault exists at the point of the movement.

Mountain Formation

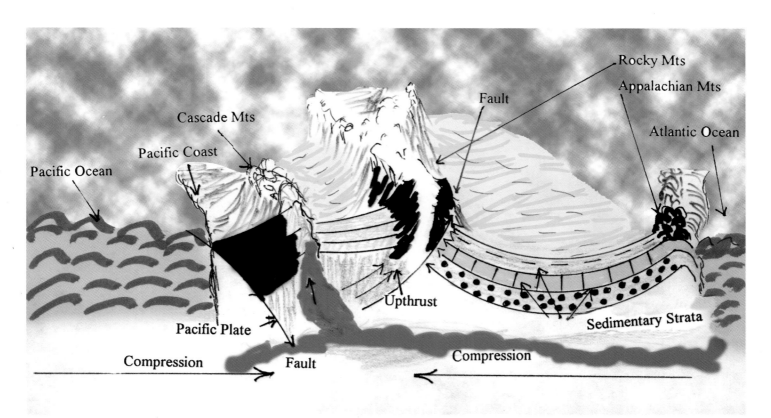

Since the beginning, the earth's crust has contorted the landscape. Then erosion smoothes down the wrinkles. The continental plates are smashing into each other and the slipping plates cause earthquakes. Fractures deep in the mantle allow magma to spew to the surface creating volcanoes both in the ocean and on land. Then glaciers and normal erosion sculpt our present terrain.

In late Triassic and early Tertiary times, the dinosaurs disappeared about the time the mountains were forming.

Tyrannosaurus Rex

The Earth Age Chart

The sequence of events of earth time is excellent for study of the Rocky Mountain Yellowstone country. The geological story is expressed in the study of rocks and fossils along with the geography. This chart shows how plant and animal life might have evolved.

In several places along the east slopes of the Rocky Mountains the earliest plant life fossils are found and also in the Beartooth, Pryor, and Big Horn Mountains, fossils of Ordovician, Devonian and Mississippian Periods are easily available for study.

Dinosaur bones are found throughout Montana and Wyoming's desert regions where the prehistoric oceans allowed growth of deciduous trees and ground plants.

During the late Cretaceous and early Tertiary Periods the mountains began forming and this event changed these swamps to forests, deserts, and life on this part of Earth.

The Earth's age chart helps explain how we think things evolved from 4.7 billions years ago up to the present time.

ERA	PERIOD	EPOCH	AGE MIL YEARS	TYPICAL PLANTS & ANIMALS
Cenozoic Age of Mammals	Quaternary	Holocene	1/100	
		Pleistocene	2	
	Tertiary	Pliocene	5	
		Miocene	24	
		Ikugicebe	37	
		Eocene	58	
		Paleocene	66	
Mesozoic Age of Reptiles	Cretaceous		144	
	Jurassic		208	
	Triassic		245	
Paleozoic Age of Fishes	Permian		286	
	Pennsylvanian		320	
	Mississippian		360	
	Devonian		408	
	Silurian		438	
	Ordovician		505	
	Cambrian		570	
Protozoic Pre-Cambrian	Younger		2500	
	Older		4700	

Montana's Yellowstone Country

Sixty million years ago the Rocky Mountains began forming.

Sedimentary stratas have been contorted by the uplifting of the mountains along the fault lines.

**Clark's Fork Fault pushing against
sedimentary plates created upturns and**

Pryor Mountain Uplift

After faulting and uplifting, came the volcanoes

Volcanoes have contributed much to the Earth's terrain during creation and up to today. Mount St. Helen before its top blew.

The volcanic activity creating Yellowstone Park came in two periods and thrust out 663 cubic miles of materials...

The eruptive process creating Yellowstone Park

The geology of the Yellowstone Park area, because of its mass, affected a major portion of the Yellowstone River drainage area.

During the rising of the Rocky Mountains this area became a high plateau, but more important was the creation of mantle fractures along the Rocky Mountain line.

The faults and fractures allowed molten lava to pool close to the surface which was responsible for major volcanic activity. The first was the Absaroka Field forming along the western side of the park and into the northwestern areas along parts of the Gallatin Range. This occurred 40 to 55 million years ago.

These eruptions covered the area with massive volumes of cinder, ash, and lavas. These events created petrified forests. The volcanic flows of rhyolite and basalt lavas covered large areas of what is now Yellowstone Park. Then erosion and glaciation affected the entire region for the next 40 million years and formed the famous Yellowstone Falls and Canyon.

Approximately 2,000 years ago began another phase of volcanic eruptions creating what is known today as the Yellowstone Park area. These eruptions continued through three phases ejecting 663 cubic miles of material out and down rivers to form the present valleys in all directions from the plateau.

Bentonite clays are found today in areas where wind-blown volcanic ash collected in shallow seas and as the compounds matured they united with the sodium of the sea water. Also, along with these large, volcanic mud flows came glacial ice dams and when they burst, boulders of granite as big as automobiles would roll down from the plateau changing whole river areas.

The remnants of these flows can be seen along the Clarks Fork, Rock Creek, and Stillwater Rivers where rounded boulders are strewn for miles along the stream banks. Smaller particles flowed on into the plains to form today's farm lands.

These sequences of events: uplifting, volcanoes, glaciers, and melting were the effective creation of America's largest wilderness area and Yellowstone Country.

The collapse of the roof materials into the caldera was the major event. This with the fractures and vents allowed mud pots, geysers, and hot springs to appear - some ten thousand in all.

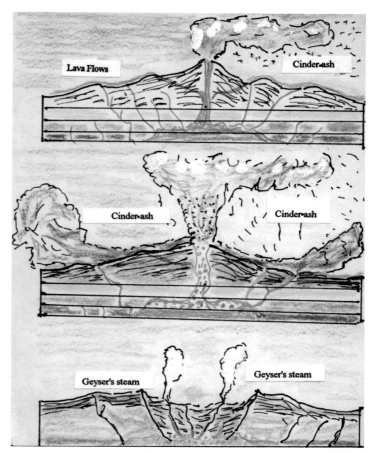

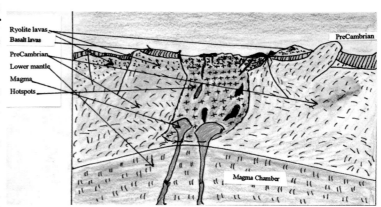

The cross-section look shows the possible hot spots and magma pools causing mud pots and geysers.

Yellowstone Plateau Area and Yellowstone Caldera

Crater Lake in the southern Oregon Cascade Mountains is an old volcanic caldera where the top was blown off and filled with water. This is an example of a volcanic crater and is approximately six miles across. The caldera of Yellowstone Park is many times larger. The volcano in Yellowstone blasted out lava and ash through many side vents. The top of the mountain fell back into the center, creating Yellowstone Park as we know it today. The fractures and vents are today's mud pots, geysers, and hot springs. The major hot spot in North America is the Yellowstone area. Hot magma in some places is only a mile beneath the surface.

The Yellowstone Park area and wilderness totals 13,000,000 acres. The Yellowstone volcano caldera is 44 miles by 33 miles and is the largest-known, single, eruptive area in the world.

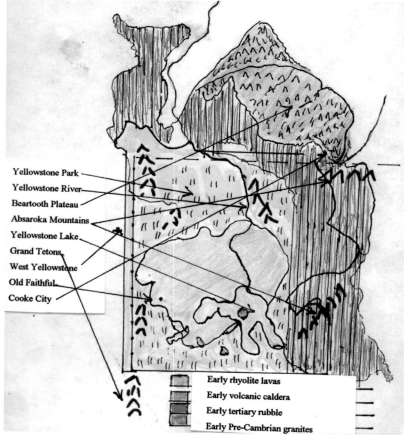

Yellowstone Park
Yellowstone River
Beartooth Plateau
Absaroka Mountains
Yellowstone Lake
Grand Tetons
West Yellowstone
Old Faithful
Cooke City

Early rhyolite lavas
Early volcanic caldera
Early tertiary rubble
Early Pre-Cambrian granites

Yellowstone Park
1872

Old Faithful

The geyser illustrates the underlying volcanic activity responsible for the formation of this magnificent mountainous area.

The Indians called this the land of many smokes. It was set aside in the 1870s as our first national park.

Yellowstone Park is...

Mammoth Hot Springs and terraces are a spectacular view south of the northern gate at Gardiner, Montana.

Super-heated water carrying dissolved calcium compounds bubbles up and spills out at Mammoth Hot Springs. The water carrying these dissolved compounds begins to cool and precipitates gather in formations to form travertine. Algae of many colors grows in the hot springs and create the multi-hued patterns in the travertine.

Rocky Mountain Goats

The Yellowstone Cutthroat Trout

This fresh water fish feeds mostly on aquatic insects and needs pure, high-oxygenated water. The pristine wilderness of the park and Rocky Mountains river systems are the only areas where these fish are still living.

The Boulder River illustrates how granite rocks flushed off the mountain plateaus help carve river bottoms.

The Mountain Region

- Beartooth-Absaroka Mountains
- The Weather
- Pryor Mountains
- Big Horn Mountains

Buckskin Billy

Modern mountain man (1906-1980), Sylvan Hart, was one of the last mountain men of the Rocky Mountain region. He raised his own food, hunted and killed game for meat and clothing which he made from skins.

Even though his time was later than the early trappers of the 1820 and 1830s, he lived as close to their lives as a hermit could.

He made his own rifles, pistols, knives, and axes, hewed timbers, and built buildings in the remote area of the Salmon River near the Montana-Idaho mountain country. He panned gold to buy powder, books, and a few other items he needed. Billy built a shop to do his metal work where he smelted copper and crafted almost every item he needed, including his gun barrels.

Buckskin Billy lived with the animals for his many years in the wilderness making semi-pets of deer, bear, a rattlesnake, toads, Big Horn sheep, a mountain lion, and others who frequented and frolicked about his little mountain area.

Please read the book, *The Last of the Mountain Men* by Harold Peterson.

Beartooth-Absaroka Mountains

Early Men of the West

They came to see the Beartooths and Absaroka mountains, the smoke country, and the beaver.

The stories told by early fur traders and explorers were often scoffed by the easterners until Thomas Moran brought back his paintings of Yellowstone Falls and surrounding scenes. Shortly after, Congress set aside Yellowstone Park in 1872.

Yellowstone River Falls
Artist, Alfred Bierstadt
Courtesy of Buffalo Bill Historical Center

The Golden Gate into Yellowstone Park
Thomas Moran 1871-72
Hayden Expedition
Courtesy of Buffalo Bill Historical Center

To the mountain men, the Yellowstone Country, the Beartooths, and Absaroka Mountains were the means to wealth, power, and a lifestyle...

The Beartooth Plateau and Absaroka Mountains

Standing on top of the Beartooth Summit just off the Red Lodge/Cooke City highway is always a wondrous view. Just how did the earth release enough energy to thrust this igneous and metamorphic block of rock upwards? This is a mystery but the compression of the continental plates may possibly be responsible. The plateau has now eroded to an average of 11,000 feet with Granite Peak standing at 12,799 feet above sea level.

The Absaroka-Beartooth wilderness is an area of 934,377 acres of few roads and spectacular mountain scenery. The granite bedrock allows each low depression to collect water from melting snows forming lakes. These lakes add glamour-like jewels on an already beautiful landscape.

The Beartooth Plateau and Absaroka Mountains

This rock exposure dates to the Pre-Cambrian Archean Era of the earth's formation. The plateau shows off 29 mountains over 12,000 feet in elevation along with some of the oldest geology exposed in the world.

After the major uplifting occurred, exposed metamorphic rocks were subject to normal erosion and during the Tertiary Period enormous volcanication took place in the southwest corner of the mountain range.

During the uplifting and movement of the mountains fractures occurred, allowing magma to flow to the surface creating mineral exposures in several areas. The minerals found are chrome, gold, platinum, palladium, and other rare metals.

The northeast portion of the uplift exposes the greatest amounts of metamorphic rock termed gneiss.

The uplift seemed to occurred in two stages: the first during the Paleocene time (60 million years ago), and the second stage in the late Miocene or early Pliocene (15 to 5 million years ago) and uplifting continues today.

The Beartooth Plateau

During the upthrusting of the Beartooth bubble, cracks and fissures occurred allowing molten igneous rock to move up to the earth's surface. This one is 50 feet wide and tops out at 8500 feet.

**Another lava dike
Gardiner, Montana**

The Beartooth Plateau and Absaroka Mountains

Beartooth Mountains

A picture study of geology, mountain scenery, still as if years ago.

The massive complex of mountains, steams, meadows, and forest are a pristine environment and pleasantly saved by the earliest of environmental acts of Congress. Yellowstone Park was the first national park created in the United States and with this action came the wilderness preservation of the Beartooth-Absaroka Mountain areas.

The age of these rocks are old Archean 3.5 billion years old

The statuesque Beartooth Butte is all that remains after erosion of the the sedimentary deposits. The Beartooth Butte shows off Ordovician dolomite, Devonian fossils, Cambrian quartzite, and other sediment now in the form of rock and exposes fossils of fish and plants 400 million years old.

Fossils of specimens of brachiopods.

Silver Tip Grizzly Bear - Rocky Mountains, Alberta, Canada
Carl Rungius
Courtesy of Buffalo Bill Historical Center

The *Grizzly Bear* has roamed throughout the Rocky Mountains and is considered the rogue of the land. His solitary nature and his style of trouble has not endeared him to living with man.

From
the
Lewis and Clark Journals
5th of May Sunday 1805
   We set out verry early and had not proceeded far before the rudder Irons of one of the Perogus broke which detained us a short time   Capt Lewis walked on shore this morning and killed a Deer,   after brackfast I walked on shore Saw great numbers of Buffalow & Elk   Saw also a Den of young wolves, and a number of Grown Wolves in every direction, The Country on both sides is as yesterday handsom & fertile. The river rising & current Strong & in the evening we saw a Brown of Grisley beare on a sand beech,   I went out with one man Geo Drewyer & Killed the bear, which was verry large and a turrible looking animal, which we found verry hard to kill   we Shot ten Balls into him before we killed him, & 5 of those Balls through his lights   This animal is the largest of the carnivorous kind I ever saw.

Beartooth-Absaroka Mountains

Geology in a capsule

The southeast fault known as the Clark's Fork Fault separated the Beartooth Range from the sedimentaries and volcanics of the Absaroka Mountains to the south.

This photo illustrates a glaciated hanging valley, a hard core of an extinct volcano and several sedimentary deposits dating back possibly 600 million years. In the far distance is the Absaroka Mountain peaks reaching over 12,000 feet.

It is important, when we view the mountains, we understand the influence on life they control.

Besides the beauty, they are the heart and soul of all around. They collect the water for summer; they add to the warmth for winter; they are the playgrounds during winter and summer; and the mountains give sanctuary to birds, insects, plants, wildlife, reserving what might be the only place left not totally changed by man's presence on this earth.

Clark's Fork Fault

39

The Absaroka/Beartooth Mountains of Montana and Wyoming are the water resource for rivers of the Big Horn, Yellowstone, Clarks Fork, Stillwater, Gallatin, Madison, Jefferson, Snake, Shoshone, Green River, and other tributaries.

Tilted sedimentary stratas

When the bubble of metamorphic rock began moving upwards, the action tipped sedimentary stratas to a nearly vertical position. These have resisted erosion and stand nearly straight skyward.

The uplifting of the mountains changed the climate. First the flora changed and then the animals evolved to fit the new country.

The change created deserts.

The

change

created

the

forests

The Forest

The quiet world of the northwest forest is often solitude. Here the trees grow so close, sunlight stays above and the ground becomes barren, covered with leaves. The deep forest is a place for plants only.

The west slopes of mountains from the Pacific Ocean to the Rockies became a plant world with a dense growth of cedars, hemlock, fir, and pine. These plants, animals did not eat.

The animals moved to the east side of the mountains where grass grew as far as the eye could see. The early prehistoric herbivores eating large volumes of plants daily changed to elk, buffalo, deer, and antelope living on grass. The early carnivores evolved to wolves, coyotes, foxes, bobcats, and badgers.

These flora and fauna changes came with the uplifting of the mountains some 60 million years ago.

So, in central North America when Lewis and Clark traversed from St. Louis to the Pacific Ocean, they wrote in journals of vast herds of buffalo, prairies full of elk, and other small game everywhere.

Even the modern Indians, Crow, Cheyenne, and Sioux who were migrating Algonquins from the northeastern coast of America, knew nothing of the giant sloths, dinosaurs, mammoth elephants, and saber-tooth tigers now extinct.

As the secrets of these mid-continental changes unfold through anthropological studies, we realize just how little our blink from the 1800s through the 1900s actually is in time.

The Mountains Create Climate

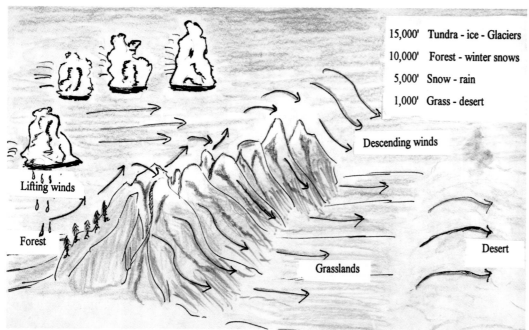

15,000' Tundra - ice - Glaciers
10,000' Forest - winter snows
5,000' Snow - rain
1,000' Grass - desert

Descending winds

Lifting winds

Forest

Grasslands

Desert

The Billings, Montana and Yellowstone River areas receive the Chinook wind effect from the descending prevailing westerly winds traveling downward from the Beartooth plateau. For every one thousand feet the air over the mountain descends to the plains, the temperature warms three degrees. The top of the plateau is about 11,000 feet while the elevation around Billings averages 3,000 feet. This air movement causes a warming of 24°. Winter temperatures can often be in the fifties.

The western faces of the Rocky Mountains create uplifting air currents creating rain, while the east sides have descending warming air creating deserts.

The mountains steal from the moisture-laden air currents traveling around the earth, especially the prevailing westerly winds, and slowly release the water, first in small streams and finally into rivers to flow out into the plains. These waters give life to the central plains of America.

The greatest resource in south central Montana and northern Wyoming is the climate.

Another Noteworthy Effect

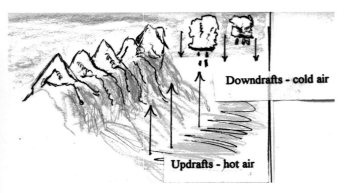

Summer thunderstorms are created by warm updrafts and, as the earth rotates, storms travel eastward across the plains. As they gain momentum, tornadoes and flash floods occur.

Warming winds called Chinooks create a milder winter climate and desert.

Captain Clark, while camped near Billings, Montana in 1806, sent Nathantel Pryor with a party of horses and men to travel over land back to the Mandan villages of North Dakota. They rode south, camping at the base of the mountains. The Crow Indians stole all of their horses the first night and the men walked back Thereafter, the mountains became known as the Pryors.

Will James

Will James, author, painter, movie star, will always be known as a man who could ride a "good" horse and tell a great story.

Many a western boy will say he read every Will James Book: *Sand, Smokey, Lone Cowboy,* etc.

The Will James ranch on the northeast corner of the Pryor Mountains, south of Billings, was as much a picture as his paintings of a horse broke in middle delivering a cowboy to the dirt. It was here he wrote many books and transferred his ideas of the west to canvas.

Montana has had many artists but Will James probably exhibited more dimension to the American public. His pencil drawings were superb; his stories were as pure as green grass; and in general, illustrated the West as we think it should be.

Will James
by *Ian Tyson*

When I was but a small boy
My father bought me many books
"bout the creatures of the river banks
And the sins of old sea cooks
But the ones I never left behind
With the old forgotten games
Were the tales of wild and windy slopes
By the man they call Will James

The living of his cowboy dreams
Or so it seemed to me
The perfect combination
Of riding high and being free

His heroes were his horses
And he drew them clear and true
On every page they'd come alive
And jump straight out at you

His race towards the sunset
Was the high and lonesome kind
Like a coyote always looking back
He left no tracks behind
So I've memorized those pictures boys
They're still the very best
If whiskey was his mistress
His true love was the west

I remember up on Dead Man Creek
Back twenty years or more
I hired on to breaking colts
Which I'd never done before
A city kid I asked myself
Now "What would Will James do?"
And you know it was the damnedest thing
But it kind of got me through

Just a few miles from the Beartooths rose the Pryor Mountains - Unique and Picturesque

The Pryor Mountains

Sometime during the period of the late Cretaceous and early Tertiary time, the Pryor Mountains were formed by faulting and compression. These exposed sedimentary rock stratas are possibly as old as Cambrian, 500 million years ago. Exposures of Devonian, Mississippian, and Pennsylvanian limestone formations are found in many places.

The Pryor Mountains are similar in age and formation to the Beartooths but still have the sedimentary layers topping the mountains and the layers are covering the Pre-Cambrian geology. The Pryors exhibit a more complete geological history from the Paleozoic through the Tertiary eras than the Beartooth Mountains.

East face of the Pryor Mountains

West side look at the uplift showing limestone plates

The Pryor Mountain Geology

The mountains allow the viewer to walk through the time capsule of 500 million years of fossils, limestone, sea beds, uplifts, fractures, and layered sediments.

Limestone bluffs east side

Limestone-eroded contortions.

East to the north look at uplifted mountains and the vertical stratas showing effect of the uplift.

The thick limestone sedimentaries are exposed across the east face; while down into the desert, islands of the red Triassic Chugwater are seen. The climate changes quickly here because of the geology. Forests grow at the upper levels, and within just a few thousand feet, sparse desert vegetation speckles the landscape.

Stacked sediment of the Chugwater formation of the Triassic Era of time.

The east side of the Pryors shows the eroded area of the Big Horn River Canyon taking its water to the Gulf of Mexico.

Pryor Mountains Climate, Vegetation, Wildlife

In the high mountains timber grows
where rainfall is enough for these plants.

At approximately 8,000 feet an unusual plant,
commonly called Rock Mat, grows on a solid
rock ledge of Devonian limestone.

*As the elevation changes from mountain top
to desert, plant life adapts to lesser amounts
of rainfall.*

Juniper tree colony makes its own environment. Life is
not kind in these semiarid, climatic zones.

The Pryor Mountains

The Pryor wild horses were probably stolen by the Indians from the Spaniards; perhaps from the Coronado expedition of the early fifteen hundreds. The Plains Indians of the central United States occupied much of Montana, Wyoming, North and South Dakota, etc. and the horses were their main source of transportation.

The Pryor Mountain horses probably escaped from the Indians. These horses have zebra stripes on the upper front legs and an extra vertebrae like the Spanish horses. They also tend to be dark gray, black, or dull brown in color. Along with the wild horses, the Pryor Mountains are home to elk, deer, bear, Big Horn sheep, and many other species.

The reward of outdoor excursions is spending the time to observe nature mutating and adapting to its environment.

The change from shallow seas of crustaceous forms of life to dinosaurs to our modern wildlife took years of adaptation.

Bull Elk

Desert Mule Deer

50

Fossils of the Yellowstone Country

Besides the fossils of clams and crustaceans, minerals like uranium, petrified wood, limestone of commercial quality, bentonite clays, pigeon-blood agate, and other interesting semi-precious rocks are found.

Some of the earliest Montana dinosaur digs occurred in the Pryors, where Deinonychus bones were found, as reported in the 1978 *National Geographic* magazine. In Eastern Montana, Triceratops and Tyrannosaurus Rex skeletons have been recovered. These earliest exposed sedimentary formations allow the study of their contents and geology.

Petrified wood limb cast

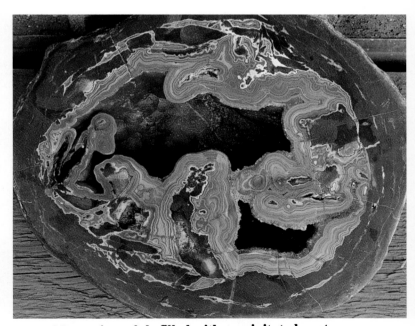

Pryor Mountain nodule filled with precipitated agate.

Big Horn Mountains

Pre-Cambrian rock pushed skyward to form Cloud Peak leaving sedimentary stratas exposed on each side.

Free Trapper
John Clymer
Courtesy of Buffalo Bill Historical Center

The mountain men were the self-sufficient, colorful adventurers of the early west.

Orodroneus Makalia dinosaur
Courtesy of Rocky Mountain Museum

The Big Horns are a large granite plateau with rugged protrusions in and around Cloud Peak.

Big Horn Mountains

This small but beautiful group of mountains lay in southeastern Montana and north central Wyoming. The Big Horns are unique in many ways. The Big Horns show off Cloud Peak at 13,167 feet above sea level, one of Wyoming's highest peaks, and some of the more spectacular exposures of sedimentary rock formations, especially on the west side where the Big Horn River Canyon cuts through the Mississippian formations.

The famous Paleo-Indian ceremonial medicine wheel on top of a high plateau in the Big Horns was put together before the modern Indians of Crows, Cheyenne, Sioux, Blackfeet.

The State of Wyoming illustrates with signs the geological features and the rock exposures as one travels across the Big Horns on highway 14A and 16. This enjoyable feature is both informational and scenic. Within a matter of hours, a viewer can drive and see Pre-Cambrian, igneous, metamorphic, Ordovician, Devonian stratas, as well as Paleozoic, Jurassic, Cretaceous of the Mesozoic, Cenozoic, and Tertiary Eras formations. The Big Horns have it all.

The rough terrain of these mountains makes them inaccessible to the public and will remain remote for years to come. The Cloud Peak Wilderness, an 189,000-acre area, is an example.

The headwaters of the Tongue River is out of the northeast area of the Big Horns and the Little Big Horn River flows off the north side of the mountains. While several small streams: Crazy Woman Creek, forks of the Powder River, and Porcupine Creek flow off the mountains.

All of these streams are excellent trout fisheries and fun for the fly fisherman.

The geology is in several parts. The core of the mountains are Pre-Cambrian metamorphic rocks age about 2.4 billion years old with sedimentary flanks. The Beartooth bubble effect pushing up the Pre-Cambrian core was the force behind the uplift. And again, climate ranges from desert to forest allowing good views of the surfaces exposed.

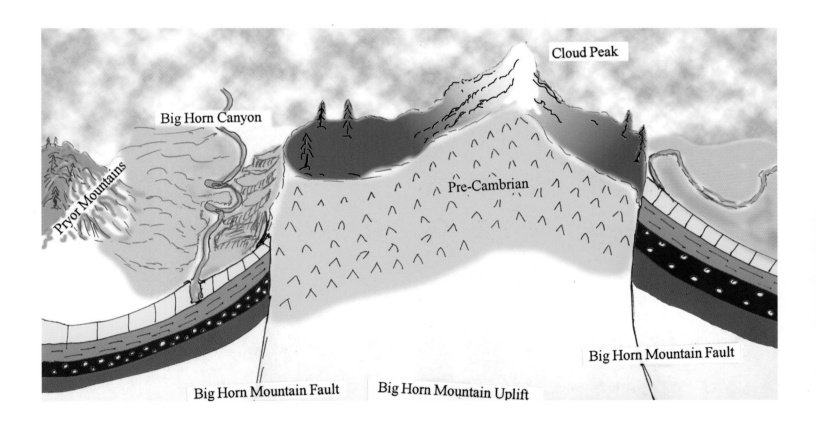

Cloud Peak

Big Horn Canyon

Pryor Mountains

Pre-Cambrian

Big Horn Mountain Fault

Big Horn Mountain Fault   Big Horn Mountain Uplift

Dan Bischoff

Northern Wyoming is desert and the Big Horn Mountains and the Absaroka Mountains break the skyline. This foreboding area was Indian country where the tribes moved in and out hunting for sustenance. But, around 1880 interest piqued for settlement in the Big Horn Basin.

At the age of 31 one noted early pioneer rancher, Dan Bischoff, sold his properties in Fountain Green, Utah. He purchased 100 cows and began trailing these animals to what is now Lovell, Wyoming.

Madison limestone

His cattle drive would take his family into some of the west's most renowned outlaw country. The east side of the Big Horn Canyon was like going back into time. Horse thieves and cattle rustlers disappeared into these canyons "breaking off" the Big Horn Mountains.

The Mississippian limestone eroded into shear rock walls harboring rattlesnakes, both human and those crawling among the boulders. This lost world was not for the timid.

Dan's early times were fraught with horse thieves, drought, and harsh winters. But Dan, being a enterprising young man, blacksmithed, owned a movie house, and started cattle ranching. His struggles began to pay off in 1919 when several farms came up for sale and he was able to homestead. Taking 640-acre homestead units for himself, his wife, and each of his three sons, as well as several neighbors, he soon began controlling thousands of acres of Big Horn Basin desert and Big Horn Mountains. He also began buying small homesteads from settlers who wanted to leave but only if they had U. S. Forest grazing units or Taylor grazing permits. Cattle ranching was his love and eventually the empire known as Bischoff Livestock was put together.

Hy and his brothers, the sons of Dan Bischoff, took over the cattle ranch after their father's accidental death and continued building the operation through the 40s, 50s, and 60s running over 2,000 head of cattle. In this desert country where it takes 75 acres of land per cow, this equates to 150,000 acres of farm, desert, and mountain lands. It took several days to ride a horse across the ranch. Much of the area lay in the remote parts of the East Big Horn Canyon where a cow might not see a cowboy all summer until fall roundup.

This area was ideal for cattle ranching. Winters in the desert were often mild and cattle could forage without the need of hay. The summers began with grazing on lower slopes of the Big Horns then as the snow melted, the cattle could move up with the growth of grass. In the fall calves were then trailed down and shipped by railroad to midwest markets.

The Bischoff ranches are in operation today owning land around Cody and Lovell, Wyoming, and Lodge Grass, Montana.

Tensleep Formation

Big Horn Mountains
Wyoming's Yellowstone Country

Big Horn snowcapped peaks

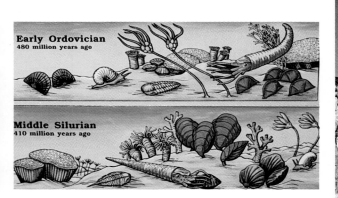

Paleo Indian Ceremonial Wheel

This painting of the famous Paleo Indian ceremonial wheel is on a bearskin and the wheel is found on the high Big Horn plateau off highway 14B.

Montana-Wyoming

The Yellowstone River Country

**Columbian mammoth prehistoric elephant
Eleven feet at the shoulders and nine tons**

**The Colby mammoth killsite, Worland,
Wyoming is where archeologists have dug
prehistoric tools and elephant bones which
are display at the University of Wyoming.**

Ordovician shale with possible worm excretions.

Big Horn Mountains

The human history of the Big Horn Mountains dates back to the prehistoric eras before glaciers and into the time of Columbian mammoth elephants. These large mammals stood eleven feet at the shoulders and weighed about nine tons.

Early Clovis Indians hunted these animals. Signs of bones, spear points, and other fossil remains are found at the Colby site where dating establishes the time about 11,500 years ago.

Moving into the modern Indian era through the 1800s, the Indians traveled in and out of the Big Horn Mountain areas hunting for big game: elk, deer, sheep, and buffalo. This region was home for the Crows, Sioux, Cheyenne, Shoshone, Arapaho Tribes.

The first whites were fur trappers so during the 1820s to the 1840s, life was fairly agreeable with the Indians. One of the most noted fur trappers and scouts was Jim Bridger and when the Bozeman Trail was opened, Jim played a major part. The Bozeman Trail was opened to allow settlers and goldminers to travel into Montana. Opening the trail was in defiance to previous treaties signed with the Sioux tribes of South Dakota, eastern Wyoming, and other areas.

The Indian resistance was directed at the white men traveling through established hunting grounds. The Bozeman Trail ran north along the east side of the Big Horns then west to Bozeman. The Indian wars and battles associated with this time were the most fiercely fought.

South of Sheridan, Wyoming, the U. S. Military fought many battles with Chief Red Cloud's Sioux over the opening of the Bozeman Trail. The trail became known as the Bloody Trail.

Today the valley is agricultural with large coal mining operations and with the beauty of the Big Horn Mountains as a backdrop, recreation and tourism add wealth.

The Big Horns were early Indian hunting grounds.

Indian hunting grounds of the Big Horn Mountains held vast herds of buffalo, antelope, and elk.

The Big Horn Basin Desert lays in the rain shadow of the Beartooths where the average rainfall is often below five inches annually.

Found at the south end of the Big Horn Basin is the giant hot springs flowing out of the Owl Mountains. The travertine deposits are colored by many species of algae growing in the hot water. The species of plants and animals able to live in the springs are being studied for medical information.

The Big Horn Basin

- Area
- Climate
- Oil, coal, bentonite and limestone
- Towns
- Thermopolis Hot Springs
- Wind River Canyon

These oil fields discovered about 1900 have pumped millions of barrels of hydrocarbons and are still pumping today.

Algae growing in the Thermopolis Hot Springs.

61

Big Horn Basin

Caroline Lockhart (1870-1962)

Caroline was a midwestern girl and began writing for the *Boston Post* at age 18. She later wrote a short story, *Orphan's Bouquet*, and became quite well known.

After being sent by the newspaper on several writing jaunts, she traveled to the Blackfeet Indian Reservation in Montana. There she met and made friends with Sourdough Sam and began trips to see the countryside.

She and Sam started a trip to McDonald's Lake in what is now Glacier Park and nearly lost her life in a big rock slide. This trip taught her how to live in the west and accept its hardships without question - even when she had a two-day ride with a man known as Kelly who was wanted for two murders in Havre, Montana.

When Caroline finally returned to the east she began to work for the New York Press. During an interview with Buffalo Bill she became enamored with his personality and stories of Wyoming. She soon gave up her New York life to return west to Cody, Wyoming. Buffalo Bill's tales drew her west again.

She became attached to Cody, Wyoming and began freelance writing about the town, the west, and the people. One article:

BANK CASHIER'S SLAYING ON DULL, DROWSY DAY SHOOK CODY COUNTRY by Caroline Lockhart. It was the afternoon of October 1, 1904 when the most sensational event in the history of Buffalo Bill's home town took place, namely the attempted robbery of the First National Bank, and the cold blooded murder of its cashier...

She became quite a man's woman about the Cody country but continued to write stories for the *Denver Post:*

WHEN THE AUTYMOBILE STRUCK TOWN - His Cayuse Clum A Telegraft Pole Declared an Old Cattleman of the Stinking Water. Saw his First Auto in Cody. by Caroline Lockhart

"Cody has gone plumb to the dogs," said the Old Cattleman of the Southfork of the Stinking Water, as he plucked an icicle from his overhanging eyebrow and laid it carefully on the stylish gilt radiator in the bar of the Irma Hotel. "It's cold up where I've been," he continued in mild explanation to 'Mine Albert' Heimer, the smoothness of whose cocktails is considered a plausible cause for a trip to Cody by the sheep and cattlemen of forty miles around. "I just met something I take for an autymobile as I was comin' up the street and my cayuse clumb a telegraft pole. It took thirty minutes of coaxing with a pair of spurs to get him down."

The townspeople of Cody feared her pen. Her stories about their lives could be a soap opera today. Cody's top society shunned Caroline but she continued to write bluntly. Even so, several of her books were made into early movies: *The Fighting Shepherdess*, starring Anita Stewart; and *The Man from the Bitterroots*, starring William Farnham.

She later bought a small ranch in the Dryhead Canyon north of Lovell, Wyoming. A lesser person could have not ranched in this desolate desert land. In spite of this she became a successful cattle rancher and was nicknamed "The Cattle Queen of the Dryhead."

Caroline Lockhart by Lucille Patrick Hicks Page 28 - Cashier Page 34 - Automobile

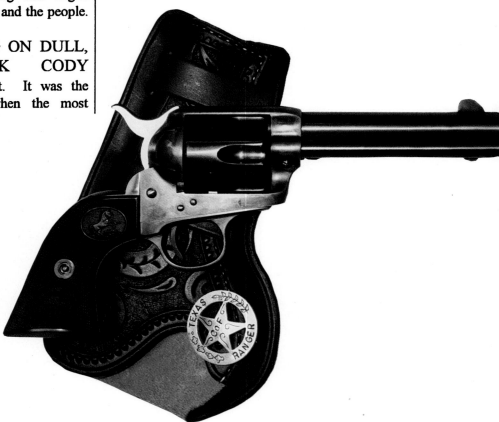

The Colt .45 was the famous shoot-out hogleg, slung off the hip. "Draw or die - your choice."

Big Horn Basin and Powder River Basin

The Big Horn Basin 120 miles long and 60 miles wide has many anticline traps collecting oil from the rising of the mountains. Some of these fields have produced millions barrels of oil.

Vast coal beds were formed in the swamps and trillions of tons lay in the Powder River Basin.

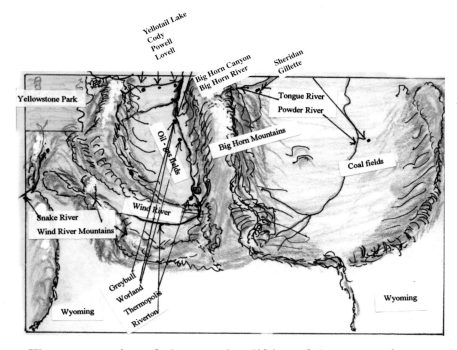

The compression of plates and uplifting of the mountains created depressions between mountain ranges, usually resulting in deserts. The major change in climate from forest to snow fields to desert effected major changes in the life living in these areas.

The dry, Wyoming deserts are sheep country

Surface mining of coal
Some seams are 150 feet thick.

Big Horn Basin Towns and Small Industry

Hauling Pryor Mountain limestone

Farmers along the Big Horn River bring their sugar beets to the Lovell, Wyoming factory.

Bentonite clays are a collection of ash from the catastrophic eruptions forming Yellowstone Park. This material has the ability to absorb water making a fine lubricant for well drilling in hard rock.

Today's Yellowstone Country business is...

The northern Wyoming area is like a rollback in time. Stop for a few minutes and visit a museum or a delightful small town.

Snowmobiling in the Big Horn Mountains

Tensleep, Wyoming

Businesses include: tourism to Yellowstone Park, cattle, farming, oil, gas, and Big Horn Mountain recreation.

Trailing cattle to the mountains

Thermopolis, Wyoming

The central portion of Wyoming is the southern area drained by the Big Horn River system. The first gathering of water flows off the slopes of the Wind River Mountains forming the Wind River and flowing into the Boysen Reservoir.

Here a prehistoric natural dam was formed by the uplift of the Owl and southern Big Horn Mountains. This is another complex geological formation area. As the Wind River enters into the Wind River Canyon, its name changes to the Big Horn River.

The complicated pushing, shoving, and uplifting of the area caused the river to work hard to carve the Wind River Canyon. This several-mile drive through the canyon shows off contorted geological formations.

The River Canyon exposes Pre-Cambrian, intrusive granites, faults and fractures, and the sedimentary layers before entering the Big Horn Basin.

The Big Horn River flows suddenly into the town of Thermopolis, home of a great mineral hot spring almost as famous as those in Yellowstone Park.

There are clues the springs were used by the early Paleo Indians and modern Indians before the mid 1800s.

The Hot Springs area was ceded to the Shoshone Tribe in 1868 and the tribe later sold this area back to the U. S. Government for a state park.

The park has two commercial swimming pools, a bath house, numerous springs, and unique view of travertine deposits.

The Big Horn Hot Springs flows 3,600,000 gallons of 130 degree water per day.

The park is approximately ten square miles. The water flows through limestone sedimentary layers on a south to north tilt out of the Owl Mountains. At its lowest depth of 6,000 feet the water temperature is 160°. As the tilted formation takes an upturn, it surfaces at 130° - perfect for a hot springs resort.

The hot water dissolves calcium carbonate as it percolates through the limestone layers and when it surfaces, the cooling water precipitates. Here the minerals collects forming delightful patterns and terraces of travertine.

Thermopolis lays at the south end of the Big Horn Basin, one of Wyoming's great natural resource areas for oil and gas. The oil fields of the Big Horn Basin producing since the early 1900s have generated several billion barrels of oil and gas.

The upturned sedimentary stratas pushed the heated water to the surface, giving Thermopolis the Big Horn Hot Springs.

Eagles nest in the wild, craggy rocks of the Wind River Canyon. The geologic limestone formations erode into rugged steep-faced cliffs.

This beautiful, pink granite intruded into fractures of darker granite found in the Wind River Canyon - the rock dates back 2.5 billion years.

The Powder River Basin is in the rain shadow of the Big Horn Mountains leaving little moisture for vegetation, but underneath the surface lays one of the greatest coal fields of the world. In some places the coal seam is 160-feet thick.

Powder River Basin

- Bozeman Trail History
- Sheridan
- Buffalo
- Big Horn Mountains

In the vast Powder River prairies, antelope dot here and there. The wild fleet-footed animals found a home here in Wyoming.

Fort Phil Kearny

The fort was burned by the Sioux but rebuilt for visitors - look around for the Indian scouts on the hills as you visit.

THE BONANZA OR BOZEMAN TRAIL

In the early 1860s there wasn't a ranch in this country from Bismarck to Bozeman and from the Platte River to Canada. To whites it was land considered "fit only to raise Indians" and while some of them were hoping for a crop failure, the majority were indifferent. They didn't care how much the tribes fought amongst themselves. They were like the old-timer whose wife was battling a grizzly bear. He said he never had seen a fight where he took so little interest in the outcome.

Then the white man's greed asserted itself and he looked for a shortcut from the Oregon Trail at Laramie, Wyoming to the gold diggin's of western Montana. The Bonanza or Bozeman Trail across Indian hunting grounds was the result. It forded the Yellowstone near here, coming from the southeast. It was a trail soaked with the blood of warriors, soldiers and immigrants. Thousands of Sioux warriors, primarily under Red Cloud, bolstered by hundreds of Cheyennes and some Arapahos, fought the trail for six years and forced its closure by the Government in 1868.

Sheridan, Wyoming

Sheridan is a small, picturesque town snuggled under the northeast corner of the Big Horn Mountains, a spot almost hidden from the rest of the world. In the town's short life, a legacy of western history has happened.

The Sioux, Cheyenne, and Crow Indians lived for several centuries in and around the area. With their horses they became nomadic following the buffalo - the animal giving food, clothing, and spirit.

Here in this rolling, hilly countryside storms flow around the north face of the Beartooths, then the Pryors, and finally the Big Horn Mountains. The mountain fronts create more rainfall growing grass to the belly of a tall horse. This area is the prized ranch land of Montana and Wyoming.

The white man saw this country as a trail to the Bozeman gold diggings but the Indians by now saw the white man for what he really was - a habitual liar and greedy beyond what they had ever previously known. He grabbed the land and called the ground his.

The Indians called these grasslands and mountains home; here herds of buffalo and elk roamed free. The wild herds provided an unending source of energy for their lifestyle.

And, from the mountains came water, first in small cascading streams, then into rivers, giving vast game herds their place under the sun.

Then the whites set their sights, first on the Bozeman Trail, which began the Sioux War. These conflicts and scrimmages were vicious. The Indians won most of the battles for the next fifteen years and closed the Bozeman Trail. When gold was discovered in the Black Hills of South Dakota, the U. S. Government abandoned the treaties signed at Fort Laramie. Troops were dispatched to protect the goldminers with a disregard for the Indian hunting grounds. Then came the railroad, next the long-horn cattle and cowboys, homesteaders and barbed wire, and cattle ranches. The Indians were soon outnumbered.

Both towns, Sheridan and Buffalo, Wyoming, have preserved their historic districts keeping intact the old western character with museums, galleries, and monuments. The countryside shows off the different battle sights of Chief Red Cloud and Chief Sitting Bull. Red Cloud was famous for the Fetterman Massacre while Sitting Bull was credited with the strategy for the famous

Battle of the Little Big Horn. General Custer split his troops. Those following Major Reno swung to the south and the soldiers with Custer traveled north to engage the Indians. Custer was caught by surprise. He and every soldier were killed. The ambush in the summer of 1876 was so successful that Sitting Bull said, "The whole battle was less time than a pipe smoke."

Six years later came the railroad and the town of Sheridan. Buffalo Bill built the Sheridan Inn next to the railroad depot and the hotel enjoyed being recognized as the "grand roadhouse" between Chicago and San Francisco.

The U. S. Government forced the Indians onto reservations and with this change came ownership of land. The Indian and the cowboy lost their free nomadic way of life. The annihilation of the buffalo herds and the coming of the homesteader brought a totally different culture to the west.

The Sheridan Inn has been beautifully renovated as part of the Heritage Center. The Inn is still "touted" as one of the finest hotels between Chicago and San Francisco.

The old Sheridan Depot now houses offices and gift shops.

Powder River Country

Travelers coming from the east on Interstate 90 and from the south on Interstate 25 find Buffalo, Wyoming, one of the gateway towns into the Big Horn Mountains. Crossing the Big Horns on the way to Yellowstone Park takes about three hours but the scenery is superb.

The ice breakup on the Tongue River

Splendid ranch country along the Big Horn Mountains.

From dinosaurs to Indians to mountain men to cowboys...

The show of the west was like no other show on earth!!

Breezy Riding

William Henry David Koerner

Courtesy of Buffalo Bill Historical Center

Bill Cody, Showman of the Old West

Buffalo Bill Poster

A. Hoen & Co., Baltimore

Courtesy of Buffalo Bill Historical Center

Western Romance and Cow Country

William "Bill" Cody

Cody put together *The Wild West Show* with Indians attacking wagon trains, shoot-outs old style, fancy roping, riding, and target shooting exhibitions.

His great characters were Sitting Bull, great Sioux chief, Annie Oakley, and real cowboys from the plains.

He finally settled in Cody, Wyoming and built the Irma Hotel, named after his daughter. The hotel remains - entertaining visitors with pictures and old-style hospitality. The old, hand-carved bar attracts visitors as it did 100 years ago.

The Buffalo Bill Historical Center in Cody, Wyoming contains one of the greatest collections of western art, Winchester rifles, and Indian artifacts in the world. This is a must stop on the way to Yellowstone Park.

Renegade Apaches
H. W. Hansen
Courtesy of Buffalo Bill Historical Center

Trailing Cattle to Montana
By Hall Diteman

The cowboy's west began when the buffalo numbers declined. They trailed cattle from Texas to Montana. The gathering of Texas cattle and trailing north continued until barbed wire was strung. The cow man today has a deeded ranch with cattle much different from those trailed up from the Pecos. The the old romantic west is still the subject of art, writing, tall tales, and movies.

The Cow Country

During the years from 1840 to 1870, the white Europeans moving into western America nearly extinguished approximately 63 million buffalo. This slaughter took many forms: shooting for meat, sport, skins and controlling the Indians.

The cow was called upon to replace these herds and supply the meat to the eastern markets. In the beginning longhorns from the mesquite brush of the Pecos in Texas were gathered and trailed up from Texas to fatten on the square miles of grass - a resource seemingly endless from the plains of Nebraska to the Cascade Mountains near the Pacific Ocean.

By now, the railroad had extended into the Plains helping to make cities like Chicago, the meat-butchering capitol of the world.

During the years of free range (1880s to 1910) the longhorns were the cattle grown in the grasslands of the west. The Montana cattle industry pushed front and center as a showcase across America.

As free range dwindled, bulls were brought from England and Europe to change the breeding of the <u>long, lean big-horned cow from Texas</u>. The severe winter of 1886-87 came early with deep snow and temperatures 60° below zero. These southern cattle died in massive numbers "waiting for a Chinook", as Charlie Russell said.

The homesteading era began about the turn of the century, 1904 to 1916, and with the land grab came barbed wire. Now with barbed wire, better breeding, raising winter feed, and controlled herds. The cowboy who followed the trail from Texas to Montana had to change with the times becoming a rancher with a spread of his own.

The cattle herds quickly changed to a beef animal; more square and broad across the back, called a Hereford, red

When the homesteader came with his plow and barbed wire, it was sunset for the loose, rambling life in the early west. The fur trapper, the Indian, and the cowboy became history.

with a white, bald face. The most famous of these cows were the Line One Breeding from Fort Keogh Experimental Station in Miles City, Montana.

As the Herefords spread and became the dominate breed from Missouri to California and New Mexico to Montana, breeding fell into a rut. The full growth of the animal was spread over several years. Calves weaned in October weighed less than 400 pounds, while a mature cow might weigh 1,200 pounds.

The industry changed, calves were sold off the cow and fed for beef in Colorado, Nebraska, Missouri, and Iowa where cheap corn was grown. The consumer market wanted the taste of fat meat.

Horse thieves should be treated like a treasure buried with care and affection.

Savvy Saying by Ken Alstad

During the 1960s and 1970s, the British Black Angus cow was introduced. This smaller animal with a black hide and black eyes matured weighing 900 to 1,000 pounds. But, his real advantage was <u>fast growth</u> with a calf weaning over 500 pounds which translated into a big profit for the rancher who might have room for only 400 to 500 cows.

Today, many of these herds in the central western states are black instead of red and white. Also, during this change crossbreeding the Herefords and Black Angus began producing a Black Baldface cow weaning calves heavier than straight Angus breeding.

Grass, as far as the eye can see

During this change, Montana became the seed stock capitol raising breeding bulls from sturdy, cold-weather animals. The pride of Montana was a natural-bred bull ready for breeding anywhere, in rough country, in cold weather, which put extra pounds on the calves and a better bottom line on the financial sheet.

The next step was further cross breeding using the Charolais bull on the Black Baldy cow now weaning calves over 600 pounds.

The new breeding was so effective at putting extra pounds of beef on the market, the production outdistanced the demand for meat during the 1980s. Calf prices dropped to an all-time low and ranchers with too much debt had to sell out.

The flip side of the coin concerned the need for even better breeding. The market wanted a bigger calf whose maturity was eleven to thirteen months weighing about 1,200 pounds.

The rancher who survived the depression of the eighties and invested in better breeding went

into the nineties making money as the numbers fell and prices per pound rose with the demand for the beef.

The industry pressures: leaner beef, tasty meat, fast-maturing calves, and a uniform meat for the marketplace are part of the struggle as this century comes to an end.

From the buffalo to the specialized beef cow took one hundred years, what a change.

The cattle industry unique as it is, does not have basic government subsidizes like wheat, barley, corn, or tobacco. So without the GOVERNMENT TINKERING, business is much more healthy. Prices fluctuate with supply and demand - the way a market-driven economy should.

Looking into the future, the cattle ranch will raise beef for a very sophisticated market, checking the meat by computer reading, and packaging a product to satisfy the American family.

> *Outlaw's stories are greatly improved by death.*

Savvy Saying by Ken Alstad

The pastoral agriculture of the western states dominates because the rough, broken lands are available only to four-footed animals able to harvest grass. Some prairies lend themselves to dryland farming of wheat, barley, and other small grains. Thus, much of the west is livestock ranches and large-acre farms with big machinery.

Cow Country

In Montana there are 1,900,000 beef cows and heifers producing beef for market. This equates to 2,166,000,000 pounds of beef annually.

A pile of meat compared to the Longhorn.

A yearling, Black Angus bull ready for sale and out to a herd of his own cows.

The Charolais cross is often the end of the breeding chain of beef for the market.

As times and enterprises changed in Montana and Wyoming, people began to come as tourists, dudes, hunters, and fishermen.

The horse was as much a part of the west as the Indian, the cowboy, or the homesteader. He was everybody's friend and slave.

You are in trouble if your neighbor's cows hang around your calf pen and bawl.

Savvy Saying by Ken Alstad

Old, abandoned, ghost towns in Montana are fun for the family to visit and imagine the events of the old west.

Middle Yellowstone

- Small Towns

- Recreation-Hunting

- Rodeo

- Ski Montana

- Billings

- Montana Agriculture

- Coal and Mining

- Oil Businesses

As the territory transformed from Indians to cowboys to ranchers, and towns, statehood was voted in 1889. With this change came politicians and Montana offered up the first woman to serve in the U. S. Congress.

Jeannette Rankin (Congresswoman, 1916) took her campaign on the road to rural Montana. She traveled the 147,000 square miles of Montana on dirt and gravel roads to become the first woman in Congress.

Jeannette Rankin

Jeannette Rankin spent her childhood in Missoula and attended college at what is now the University of Montana. She entered college in 1902 and graduated with a degree in biology. For several years she taught school and worked as a social worker.

In 1920 while completing graduate work at the University of Washington, the cause of women's right to vote came to the forefront. In Washington State she fought and helped win the battle for women's right to vote then moved back to Montana to carry the torch for the same cause.

During her childhood as a ranch girl and choreperson for her family she realized the state of American women. They were not to go to college, hold financial positions, or vote.

Jeannette realized in order to effect change she needed to be a congresswoman. Montana was a large, rural state with roads of gravel, narrow, and difficult. Her best friend and brother, Wellington, became her campaign manager and they motored to every outpost in the state. The rest is history.

In 1916 Jeanette Rankin became the first woman in the U. S. Congress. She stood firmly against war, for women's rights, and worked hard for social reform of child labor, poverty, etc.

Her vote against World War I did not bode well in Montana and she lost her next election. Her position against war was "You can no more win a war than you can win an earthquake." She again ran for Congress in an attempt to keep the United States out of World War II and was elected to the House in 1940. After the attack on Pearl Harbor she was truly in the minority with her "no" vote to war against Japan. But she stood by her vote and her election promise to keep America out of war knowing the unpopular position would again cost her re-election.

During her eightieth year she led a march on Washington to stop the Viet Nam War. This attention demonstrated many Americans were against the political Viet Nam War. The negative feelings of the people escalated against Lyndon Baynes Johnson, U. S. President, who contrived the Bay of Tonkin incident to escalate the conflict. The war was a political engagement rather than a fight for a cause.

Jeanette Rankin's statues stands in the Montana capitol and in Washington, D. C. and is inscribed: "I cannot vote for war."

Travel...Small Towns Montana

After traveling out of the mountains and through the park and the upper Wyoming basins and along the river, we find small towns in Montana.

Gardiner, Montana
Gateway to the Yellowstone Park

Down the river we find...

Travel...Small Towns Montana

...Livingston

...Big Timber

...Columbus

Livingston, Montana

Big Timber, Montana

Columbus on the Yellowstone

Montana small towns offer a special kind of easy living for the family. Hunting and fishing are out the back door. Skiing is minutes away and travel into the backcountry is without traffic jams. New businesses locating here find a well-educated and stable work force.

...Red Lodge
...Forsyth
...Miles City

Red Lodge, Montana, is now a spiffy, attractive, western, small town, fun to visit and browse enroute to the Beartooths.

Forsyth is a sleepy small town along I94 to visit for a reminder of the old west.

Miles City: Cow country and bucking horses

Life in rural Montana means: more time each day to enjoy living.

Some Montana towns were so small when the train pulled into the station, it was out of town.

Visit for recreation.

From history to the present people and activities...

Recreation Industry

Recreation available in the Yellowstone River system has something for everyone: fly fishing, pack trips, mountains of scenic splendor, browsing in small towns and viewing rimrocks against a clear, big sky. Tourists find interesting sights and nooks to visit. The area is the northern gate to Yellowstone Park through Cooke City, Gardiner, or West Yellowstone. Finding time to visit Montana will be fun for the family.

A flowering meadow and wild iris.

Stellar Jay

Today's Yellowstone Country is...

Fly fishing

Yellowstone Country Rivers

- Upper Yellowstone
- Boulder
- Stillwater
- Clark Fork
- Big Horn
- Tongue

The Mayfly

Just dabble a small mayfly behind the rock

Six pounds of everything a fisherman needs

Fly fishing Montana's blue ribbon trout streams are superb recreation drawing flycasters from all over the world.

A five-pound rainbow trout taken by dry fly is the dream of dreams.

The fly fisherman prides himself as "The Sportsman."

Recreation is business...

Hunt Montana...

as did the Indians of yesterday. Today, they come from the east, south, and midwest to scout through the rimrocks for game.

In the Foothills
Carl Rungius
Courtesy of Buffalo Bill Historical Center

Winchester found a gold mine with the 30-30 lever action saddle gun. Many western men own at least one of these rifles.

Yellowstone Country is back country.

The Mountaineers - Big Horn Sheep on Wilcox Pass
Carl Rungius
Courtesy of Buffalo Bill Historical Center

*While you
are here,
stop for
other fun.*

Mule Deer in the Badlands
Dawson County, Montana
Carl Rungius
Courtesy of Buffalo Bill Historical Center

The Rocky Mountain Big Horn sheep are the trophies of the mountains. Once near extinction are now back in reasonable numbers again.

Guide services are available for pack trips into the wilderness for fishing, hunting, photo trips, and visiting the outdoors. Total revenues for Montana Fish and Game Department in 1994 were $42,285,181 of which licenses were $24,642,196.

The Rodeo

The recreational rodeo originating from the Fourth of July picnics has grown into a circuit business. Professional cowboys travel from town to town for prize money, roping, racing, and riding bucking horses and bulls, and is now a year-round business.

The bronc rider is having an early payday "dirt."

Bull riding is the toughest of all sports

Ski
Montana...

Red Lodge Mountain

Skiing, snowmobiling, and cross-country activities are fun. Here one finds Montana and Wyoming at their best...

Big Horns, Pryors, Beartooths, Crazys, and Bridgers - just waiting.

Come...

And, while visiting, stop for a time in Billings - Hub of South Central Montana.

Billings, Montana

The *Yellowstone River* flows into the city of Billings from the west, pushing against the east bluffs, then turns north to travel eastward.

In some *prehistoric time the bluffs and glaciers* dammed the river creating a lake backing 50 miles upstream. Small rounded gravel is on top of the bluff some 600 or 700 feet high, showing an early lake shore.

The river finally drained this lake leaving a fine river bottom for agriculture. When the mountains rose and created the climate, this area along the *Yellowstone River was given gentle seasons with summers allowing corn and sugar beets to grow. Winters are mild with*

descending Chinook winds melting snow almost as it falls. Even when Canadian cold seeps down from the north, these winds push back the cold allowing Billings a mild wintertime.

As the glaciers melted and the lake drained, the valley floor filled with grass and cottonwood trees which lined the stream banks from Livingston to the Missouri.

The railroad was moving westward fast in the 1880s expecting to be in the Billings area in 1883. A nearby town, Colter, was a rough frontier post not attractive by reputation to the railroad heads who had asked and received a 1,200-acre grant to start the town of Billings, Montana. *The town officially began in 1882 to flourish into the now 120,000 population serving south central Montana.*

The city became the hub servicing the vast area with medical centers, distribution centers, central shopping services for south central Montana and northern Wyoming.

Fly in on United,, Delta, Northwest and Horizon Air.

Logan International Airport

First Interstate Building

Annually Billings averages 219 days of sunshine, about 15 inches of rainfall and enjoys a milder climate than Chicago, Minneapolis, or Calgary...

Billings is the service center for the Yellowstone area:

- *Medical - the most advanced service of the four-state area is here with two major hospitals*
- *Recreation - the Metra is a multi-use facility for sports, fairs, rodeos, concerts, ice shows, horse racing, etc.*
- *Education - educational facilities are available with public and private schools and four-year systems.*
- *Commerce - railroad, trucking, air transportation, and the major distribution center of foods.*

Moss Mansion

Deaconess hospital complex

The Deaconess-Billings Clinic Health System serves the entire region of the Yellowstone River Country and more.

Their doctors give specialized medical care by charter aircraft to the towns of Glendive, Sheridan, Powell, Cody, etc. to assist outlying clinics .

These satellite facilities offer rural areas full cardiac, orthopedic, and twenty other fully-extended services of the feature center in Billings, Montana making the Yellowstone area a better place to live.

Preston Moss, an eastern man, stepped into the history of Billings in 1902. He liked the town and country and moved his family to this frontier land. He became a leading citizen who dabbled in most of the businesses: hotels, banks, heat, power, and irrigation. Among his prized entrepreneurial endeavors was the starting of the Billings Sugar Company which even today infuses 140,000 million dollars into the economy.

He hired Henry Janeway Hardenburgh to design his new home. Henry was the leading architect of his time and famous for the building of the Waldorf-Astoria Hotel in New York, the Willard Hotel in Washington, D.C., and many others. The Moss Mansion is listed on the National Register of Historic Places.

View of part of the Metra complex

Also, Billings is the central area of agriculture for the Yellowstone Country...

Montana's Agriculture

- The semi-arid grass prairies from Nebraska to the Rockies receive adequate rainfall most years for crops like wheat and barley, sometimes just enough.
- But, as the prairies were turned from sod to dryland farms through the Homestead Acts of the early 1900s, the west changed.
- Farmers began raising enough bread grains to feed the world.
- They could start their tractors, head north until noon, turn, and travel south until sunset and start again the next day on the same piece of farm ground.
- The acres seemed to stretch to the far horizon and farming became big tractors pulling enough machinery behind to do all phases of the tilling at one pass.
- The government became involved in price supports and control and the farmers worked harder to produce more wheat per family unit with bigger and better machinery.
- It was the story of the dog chasing its tail.
- Irrigated farm size was controlled by water availability, but the vast dryland farms became bigger and bigger.
- When the world population catches up with farm production, the economics will change.

The Yellowstone River valley experiences a climate favorable for agricultural crops.

Immense silos store grain

Dryland crop farming is hope and tomorrow.

Montana Agriculture is Big

The two major sugar-producing companies of Montana and northern Wyoming are Western Sugar Company and Holly Sugar Company.

The railroad promoted the sugar business in the very early 1900s in the Billings, Montana area. Today, Western Sugar gives contracts to beet growers from Forsyth to Belfry in Montana and in Wyoming along the Big Horn River.

Holly Sugar Company is located in Worland, Wyoming and Sidney, Montana and Western Sugar is in Lovell, Wyoming and Billings, Montana.

Producing sugar in the state is one of the few value-added ag industries. The dry desert country with hot summers is ideal for this crop. Farm yields are as high as 30 tons per acre with an average sugar content of 17.6%.

A beet-growing contract is a bonus to a good farmer in the Yellowstone Valley. In 1994, approximately 140 million dollars flowed from 68,720 Montana acres.

Western Sugar gathers beets from farms up and down the Yellowstone River and Clarks Fork, Big Horn, etc. tributaries.

The Holly Sugar factory in Worland, Wyoming is value-added economics for the Big Horn Basin

The Triceratops dinosaur roamed eastern Montana.

The dinosaur fossils are a reminder of the real economic resources of the area. Coal is plant fossils collected in layers and oil is cooked liquid drained from marine shales.

Montana-Wyoming Resource Industries

Coal Mining

Mining is an extractive industry often leaving scars on the landscape. Old mining areas such as Butte and Anaconda Montana are still sore spots, but holding ponds, replacing the top soil, and other means are forming a more receptive attitude toward mining.

We live in a world where we like our toys: autos, airplanes, appliances, electricity, photographs, the list goes on... Therefore, mining for metals, coal, oil, and minerals are integral to this economy.

It is often a stretch to have happiness for the extractor, the user, and the preservationist.

The coal reserves in Montana and the surrounding states are in trillions of tons. Montana sells about 250 million tons of coal to utilities in the midwest and eastern markets. In 1994 this grossed 324 million dollars leading the mining income for the state.

Coal mining began when the railroads used coal to drive engines. Red Lodge and Roundup, Montana were early coal mining towns providing coal for the railroads. Today, the coal is mined with giant shovels and loaded into railroad cars to travel to midwestern utilities for the manufacture of electricity for towns, cities, and industry.

Here at Westmoreland's Absaloka Sarpy Creek mine, the overburden is stripped, set aside, and the coal is loaded into unit railroad train cars holding 12,000 tons of coal per trip to eastern markets.

This shovel takes the overburden off the coal layers and moves approximately 115 cubic yards per scoop.

Coal mining is a volume business moving millions of tons of coal per year.

The Absaroka Mountains fractured during their formation and often allowed rich magma to surface.

The Stillwater Mine processing plant

The pristine Stillwater River running below the mine operation is protected from chemical contamination. The river is a favorite trout stream for summer fly fishing.

Stillwater Platinum-Palladium Mine

The richest deposits of platinum and palladium metals are found in the Stillwater complex.

The Stillwater Mining Company mills 2,000 tons of these ores daily which results in annual sales of 220,000 ounces of platinum and 720,000 ounces of palladium to a hungry market of electric conductors and catalytic converters.

This is the only source for these metals used in United States industry. Now, as foreign countries are asking their auto industries to use catalytic converters and as the micro-circuitry of the computer industry expands, the demand for these metals grows daily.

The Stillwater geological complex stretches across the north face of the Beartooth Mountains from Nye to Big Timber, Montana.

The geology of this rock complex is old igneous rock formed in horizontal pools and stratas far beneath the crust of the earth. The magma cooled and the minerals and metals separated in layers taking many years to happen. The Stillwater Mining Company is taking only the layer containing platinum and palladium which extends some twenty-eight miles across the face of the mountains. The other stratas will be mined when prices are more favorable.

When the Rocky and Beartooth Mountains began uplifting from the shallow seas, the horizontal layers of igneous Stillwater complex were tilted 45 to 70 degrees, nearly vertical, and exposed these 2.7 billion-year-old rock veins of precious metals.

The mining operation employs 600 and adds 125 million dollars to the Montana and U. S. economy.

The importance of this mining complex to our economy cannot be underestimated as this geologic formation is exposed in only a very few places in our world. The Stillwater complex is one of the richest known deposits of the platinum group of metals.

Note the crystals of precious metals in the ore.

The Oil and Natural Gas Industry

Our third president, Thomas Jefferson, dreamed of a waterway or canal from the upper Missouri to the Columbia River to the Pacific Ocean but it was never a reality. The Rocky Mountains were too high and too wide.

But eighty years after the Louisiana Purchase the iron horse with steam blowing crossed the continent. The railroad arrived at Billings, Montana in 1883 ending the river boats on the Missouri and Yellowstone and gave the western United States its boost to boom. Along with the main lines came other railroads such as the Milwaukie Road. When the Milwaukie Road arrived at Lavina, Montana, the old western cow and sheep town was changed from that moment on.

Ludwig (Louie) Lehfeldt, operated a large sheep ranch from the Musselshell River to the Snowy Mountains and also owned the freight and stage line from Billings to Lavina. When Louie learned the railroad was coming, he sold a large piece of his ranch to John Quincy Adams whose land company was connected to the Milwaukie Road.

John Adams paid Louie $100,000 and moved Lavina closer to the railroad and deeded some of the land back to the town of Lavina. He also gave Louie a few acres to build a hotel. Louie built the hotel in 1908 and in honor of his new friend named the hotel "The Adams." John Adams came to the dedication and presented Louie a gift of a red, brass-trimmed Maxwell automobile. This was a beautiful machine and one of the first autos to come to Montana. The Adams Hotel with the red Maxwell parked in front became famous as a bed and meal stop in Montana. Today, there are no red Maxwells running around but the

vast expanse of Montana demands travel by auto. The vehicle sales for 1995 in Montana totaled 463,400,000 dollars. This coupled with production and sales of gas and oil is a leading income producer for both Montana and Wyoming.

Here in the Yellowstone Country oil men speak of the Mission Canyon, Red River, or Lodgepole as if they were just over the next hill. But they are drilling for oil to depths of 12,000, 14,000 or maybe 16,000 feet below the surface. This equates to two, three, or four miles to find subterranean treasures hidden in some pool collecting hydro-carbon liquids.

The Montana and Wyoming oil and gas fields are the result of the creation of the Rocky Mountains and other related mountain groups.

During the Triassic, Jurassic, and Cretaceous Periods of lowland swamps in central North America, vast coal beds were forming from plant residue collecting in broad layers. Also, the shallow seas gave us marine shales formed from algae, plankton, and diatoms creating our oil reserves.

When the Pacific and continental plates began compression and pushing mountains upwards, this also created anticlines and synclines, usually on the east sides of these mountain ranges. These traps, where tilts and uplifts allowed these liquids to collect, are called Red River, Mission Canyon, and other stratas.

Oil, being much like gold, is where you find it, but the basins east of the Rockies is a great area where oil men have been hunting since the early 1900s.

Three major petroleum companies Conoco, Exxon, and Cenex built refineries in Billings and Laurel.

The Conoco Refinery

The Adams Hotel

Stratigraphic correlation chart

ERA	PERIOD	BIG HORN BASIN	SOUTH CENTRAL MONTANA	NORTHERN POWDER RIVER BASIN	WILLISTON BASIN
CENOZOIC	TERTIARY	FORT UNION FM: TONGUE RIVER MBR, LEBO MBR, TULLOCK MBR		WASATCH FM; FORT UNION GP: TONGUE RIVER MBR, LEBO MBR, TULLOCK MBR	FLAXVILLE FM; FORT UNION FM: TONGUE RIVER MBR, LEBO MBR, TULLOCK MBR
MESOZOIC	CRETACEOUS (Upper)	LANCE FM; LENNEP FM; MEETEETSE FM; JUDITH RIVER FM / PARKMAN SS; CLAGGET FM; EAGLE FM (VIRGELLE SS); CODY FM / TORCHLIGHT SS; FRONTIER FM / PEAY SS (MESA VERDE GP / COLORADO GP)	HELL CREEK FM; FOX HILLS FM; BEARPAW FM; JUDITH RIVER FM; CLAGGET FM; EAGLE FM (VIRGELLE SS); TELEGRAPH CK FM; NIOBRARA FM; CARLILE FM / FRONTIER (MONTANA GP / COLORADO GP)	HELL CREEK FM; FOX HILLS FM; BEARPAW FM; JUDITH RIVER FM (PARKMAN SS); CLAGGET FM; EAGLE FM (SHANNON SS); TELEGRAPH CK FM; NIOBRARA FM; CARLILE FM (MONTANA GP / COLORADO GP)	HELL CREEK FM; FOX HILLS FM; BEARPAW FM; JUDITH RIVER FM; CLAGGET FM; EAGLE FM; TELEGRAPH CK FM; NIOBRARA FM; GREENHORN FM (MONTANA GP / COLORADO GP)
	CRETACEOUS (Lower)	MOWRY FM; MUDDY SST; SKULL CK SH; DAKOTA SILT; GREYBULL FM; KOOTENAI FM; LAKOTA FM (CLOVERLY GP)	GREENHORN FM; BELLE FOURCHE / BIG ELK; MOWRY FM; SKULL CK SH; DAKOTA SILT; DAKOTA FM / GREYBULL SS; KOOTENAI FM; LAKOTA FM	GREENHORN FM; BELLE FOURCHE FM; MOWRY FM; MUDDY SS; SKULL CK SH; DAKOTA SILT; DAKOTA FM; FUSON FM; LAKOTA FM	BELLE FOURCHE FM; MOWRY FM; SKULL CK SH; DAKOTA FM; KOOTENAI FM (FUSON); LAKOTA FM
	JURASSIC	MORRISON FM; SUNDANCE FM (UPPER MBR, LOWER MBR); GYPSUM SPRINGS FM	MORRISON FM; SWIFT FM; RIERDON FM; PIPER FM (ELLIS GP)	MORRISON FM; SUNDANCE FM (UPPER MBR, LOWER MBR); GYPSUM SPRINGS FM	MORRISON FM; SWIFT FM; RIERDON FM; PIPER FM (PIPEROCK MBR, TAMPICO MBR); NESSON FM (KLINE MBR, POE MBR) (ELLIS GP)
	TRIASSIC	CHUGWATER FM; DINWOODY FM	CHUGWATER FM; DINWOODY FM	SPEARFISH FM	SPEARFISH FM; PINE SALT
PALEOZOIC	PERMIAN	PHOSPHORIA FM	PHOSPHORIA FM	PHOSPHORIA FM / OPECHE FM / MINNEKAHTA FM	MINNEKAHTA FM; OPECHE FM
	PENNSYLVANIAN	TENSLEEP FM; AMSDEN FM; DARWIN SS	TENSLEEP FM; AMSDEN FM	TENSLEEP FM; MINNELUSA; AMSDEN FM	MINNELUSA FM; TYLER FM
	MISSISSIPPIAN	MADISON GROUP	MADISON GP (MISSION CANYON LS, LODGEPOLE LS); CHARLES FM	CHARLES FM; MADISON LS	HEATH FM; OTTER FM; KIBBEY FM; CHARLES FM; MADISON GP (MISSION CANYON LS, LODGEPOLE LS, BAKKEN FM)
	DEVONIAN	THREE FORKS FM; JEFFERSON FM; BEARTOOTH BUTTE FM	THREE FORKS FM / BIRDBEAR; JEFFERSON FM / DUPEROW; BEARTOOTH BUTTE FM	THREE FORKS FM; JEFFERSON FM	THREE FORKS FM; BIRDBEAR (NISKU) FM; DUPEROW FM; SOURIS RIVER FM; DAWSON BAY FM; PRAIRIE EVAPORITE; WINNIPEGOSIS FM; ASHERN FM (JEFFERSON GP / ELK POINT GP)
	SILURIAN			INTERLAKE FM	INTERLAKE FM; STONEWALL FM
	ORDOVICIAN	BIG HORN FM (LEIGH DOL, LANDER MBR)	BIG HORN FM (LEIGH DOL, LANDER MBR)	BIG HORN FM; STONY MTN FM; RED RIVER FM; WINNIPEG FM	STONY MTN FM (GUNTON MBR, STOUGHTON MBR); RED RIVER FM; WINNIPEG FM
	CAMBRIAN	GALLATIN LS SNOWY RANGE; PILGRIM FM; GROS VENTRE GP; FLATHEAD SS	GROVE CK FM; GALLATIN LS SNOWY RANGE; GROS VENTRE GP; FLATHEAD SS	GROVE CK FM / DEADWOOD; GROS VENTRE GP; FLATHEAD SS	DEADWOOD FM
PRECAMBRIAN	PROTEROZOIC	PRE-BELT ROCKS	PRE-BELT ROCKS	PRE-BELT ROCKS	PRE-BELT ROCKS
	ARCHEAN	PRE-BELT ROCKS	PRE-BELT ROCKS	PRE-BELT ROCKS	PRE-BELT ROCKS

Field notes

BIG HORN BASIN:
- S. CLARK'S FK, ELK BASIN & NW, LINE CK
- BELFRY, S. CLARK'S FK., DEAN DOME, NW ELK BASIN, JACK CK, MACKAY DOME
- CLARK'S FORK
- MACKAY DOME, ROSCOE DOME
- N. CLARKS FORK
- ELK BASIN
- ELK BASIN, NW ELK BASIN, FRANNIE
- ELK BASIN, NW ELK BASIN, FRANNIE
- ELK BASIN
- ELK BASIN

SOUTH CENTRAL MONTANA:
- DRY CREEK, GOLDEN DOME, RAPELJE
- LAKE BASIN & N., RAPELJE
- DRY CK, GOLDEN DOME, LAKE BASIN & N., RAPELJE
- PARK CITY
- LAKE BASIN
- DRY CK, GOLDEN DOME, LAKE BASIN & N.
- CROOKED CK, LAUREL, MOSSER
- DRY CK & W. GOLDEN DOME
- DRY CK

NORTHERN POWDER RIVER BASIN:
- ASH CK
- LISCOM CK, PUMPKIN CK
- BELL CK, LEARY, ROUGH CK, WRIGHT CK
- SE BELL CK, HAMMOND
- LODGEGRASS, SOAP CK, E. SOAP CK, SNYDER
- SOAP CK
- SOAP CK

WILLISTON BASIN:
- CEDAR CK, PLEVNA
- CEDAR CK, GASLIGHT, PLEVNA, THREE MILE
- EAST POPLAR
- E. COW CK, WELDON
- ANVIL, BAINVILLE, BENRUD, BLACK DIAMOND, BRORSON, E BURGET, CANAL, CATTAILS, CLEAR L., COMERTOWN, COW CK, DEER CK, DIVIDE, DOOLEY, DWYER, EAGLE, FAIRVIEW, FLAT L., FT GILBERT, GOOSE L., GUNSIGHT, LONG CK, LUSTRE, MIDFORK, MINERAL BENCH, MONDAK, NOHLY, POPLAR, PRAIRIE ELK, RICHEY, RIDGELAWN, RIPRAP, SHOTGUN CK, VOLT, WODOROW
- BIG MUDDY CK, BRORSON, BURGET, CABIN CK, CANAL, E, CROCKER SPGS., EAGLE, FAIRVIEW, FLAXVILLE, FT GILBERT, GAS CITY, GUNSIGHT, HAY CK, KATY L., LONE BUTTE, LOOKOUT BUTTE, LUSTRE, MEDICINE L., MONARCH, W. MONDAK, NORTH FORK, PENNEL, PINE, PUTNAM, RED BANK, RIDGE LAWN, SECOND CK, SIDNEY, SIOUX PASS, SOUTH FORK, SUNNY HILL, TARGET, THREE BUTTES, VAUX
- BRORSON, N. CHARLIE CK, COMERTOWN, EAGLE, N, ENID, GIRARD, W. MONDAK, OUTLOOK & S., PUTNAM, SALT LAKE, SPRING LAKE, STAMPEDE, TWO WATERS, VAUX
- E. CHARLIE CK, COMERTOWN, CRANE, DWYER, EAGLE, FT GILBERT, MEDICINE L., MINERAL BENCH, OLLIE, S. OTIS CK, OUTLOOK, RAYMOND, RED WATER, RIDGELAWN, SECOND CK, SPRING L., STAMPEDE, SUNNY HILL, TWO WATERS, WOODROW, YATES
- ANVIL, E & NE, BENRUD, BLACK DIAMOND, CARLYLE, CHARLIE CK & N., CHELSEA CK & CLEAR L., COLORED CANYON, COMERTOWN & S, DWYER FLAT L., W. LONG CK, NINEMILE, NOHLY, OUTLOOK, PALOMINO, RAYMOND & NE, RED FOX, SALT LAKE, N. SIOUX PASS, SPRING L., TULE CK, S. & E., VOLT, WAKEA
- BLOOMFIELD, LOST CK, SW RICHEY, ROYALS, VAUX
- ANVIL, N. BAINVILLE, FAIRVIEW & E, HONKER, MEDICINE L., OTTER CK, OUTLOOK & W. RAYMOND, RESERVE, RUSH MOUNTAIN, SINGLETREE, N.SIOUX PASS, WAKEA
- N. BAINVILLE, BIG MUDDY CK, BLOOMFIELD, CABIN CK, CRANE, DEER CK, EAGLE, GLENDIVE, HAY CK, LOBO, LOOKOUT BUTTE, MEDICINE L., W. MONDAK, OUTLOOK, PENNEL, PINE, PRONGHORN, PUTNAM, RESERVE & II, SW RICHEY, SAND CK, SIOUX PASS, VAUX, VIDA, WAKEA, WOODROW
- BAINVILLE & N, BIG MUDDY CK, BRORSON, BRUSH L., BURNS CK, CABIN CK, CANAL, CARLYLE, CHARLIE CK, CLEAR L & S, COMERTOWN, CULBERTSON, CLIPTON, DEER CK, FAIRVIEW, FERTILE F, FT GILBERT, FOUR MILE CK, FOX CK, FROID, GAS CITY, GIRARD, GOOSE L, HAY CK, KATY L, KRUG CK, L. BEAVER, LONE BUTTE, LONETREE, LOOKOUT, OLLIE, OTIS CK & E, OUTLOOK, OXBOW, PENNEL, PINE, PRONGHORN, PUTNAM, RAINBOW, RAYMOND, RED BANK, RED WATER, REFUGE, REPEAT, RESERVE, RICHEY, RIVER BEND, ROCKY POINT, RUSH MTN, SALT L., SAND CK, SECOND CK, SIDNEY, SIOUX PASS, SOUTH FORK, SPRING L., STAMPEDE, SUNNY HILL, THREE BUTTES, TWO WATERS, VAUX, WAKEA, WINDMILL, WODOROW, WRANGLER, YATES

(Notations at right margin: Mission Canyon FM; Lodge Pole FM; River; Red River)

SOME FIELDS OMITTED DUE TO SPACE LIMITATIONS

Drilling depths are dependent upon where the strata is found above the Pre-Cambrian basement rock. Red River may be found from 10,000 to 16,000 feet below the surface.

Lower Yellowstone

- ◆ **Agriculture**
- ◆ **Miles City**
- ◆ **Glendive**
- ◆ **Sidney**
- ◆ **Oil and Gas**
- ◆ **Paddle Fish**
- ◆ **Desert**

Rivers produced the badlands near Glendive, Montana

The geologic history of Region Seven, lower Yellowstone Valley, includes inland seas and brackish delta swamps which formed coal beds and collected liquid hydro-carbons as they formed in the marine shales.

The rising of the mountains and early volcanic activity allowed volumes of materials to cover eastern Montana and western North Dakota.

As the continental plate compressed some rising of the eastern Montana areas occurred creating hills and ridges. The rivers flowing eastward deposited tons of cinder and ash and other eroded materials into low spots, canyons, and other collective areas. This created the badlands of the Miles City, Glendive, and the Little Missouri areas of Montana and western North Dakota.

During early prehistoric times, the Missouri River ran north to the Hudson Bay Drainage of Canada. But, in the last 10,000 years when glaciers pushed down from the Arctic, their influence changed the course of the Missouri River. It now flows in a southeastern direction to join the Mississippi River and gather the Yellowstone and Little Missouri Rivers to flow to the Gulf of Mexico.

When the glaciers melted they left scrapings of rocks, gravel, and soil over a large portion of

northern Montana and North Dakota, also influencing the landscape.

The broken, scabby-hill landscapes of eastern Montana and western North Dakota are a result of the ice blocks from the north and the melting of the glaciers feeding off the Rocky Mountains. Also affecting the materials coming eastward was the eruptive processes of the Yellowstone volcano pushing tons of cinder and ash skyward to float on the prevailing westerly winds to settle over these escarpments.

The three major influences are uplifting of the mountains, glaciers from the north, and volcanic residue from the west. They all helped create a harsh looking area of the lower Yellowstone Drainage.

The river bottom wandering from Billings to the mouth is where young soils have been deposited and is the agricultural area of Region Seven.

The Missouri River Paddle Fish is a remnant of the prehistoric polyodon spathula dating back millions of years. The fish uses its long snout (about two-feet long) to hunt through the mud to unearth microscopic organisms. Caviar from these fish is sold in gourmet stores.

Region Seven lays in what is known as the Williston oil and gas geologic region which is Montana's major production area. The drilling depth for this resource is down to the Mission Canyon, Lodgepole, and Red River formations.

The oil and gas industry drills, pumps, refines, and distributes to serve broad, everyday, market needs.

Lower Country Along the Yellowstone
Agriculture

- ◆ Wheat
- ◆ Hay
- ◆ Corn
- ◆ Beets
- ◆ Cattle
- ◆ Sheep

Although the earth's color is not black as the midwest's, the mineral-rich prairie needs only water to give excellent yields of wheat, barley, corn and beets.

Northeastern Montana

The northeastern section of Montana was homesteaded in the early 1900s and many of the same families remain on the land today raising cattle, wheat, and barley.

The railroad pushed away the river boats about 1880 and is still the major carrier of coal and wheat.

Grain elevators are often small-town centers.

A coal-powered electrical plant Montana-Dakota Utility Sidney, Montana

Fossilized mammoth tusk found near Glendive.

Conclusion

- Crafts
- Rocks
- Desert
- Ending

As you travel through the Yellowstone Area, look for handicrafts, rocks, and fossils for memories.

Montana metals include gold for chains and brackets, silver for bangles, copper for industry, and jasper and sapphires for rings.

Finding Rocks of Geologic Times

The mountains in the Yellowstone country are unique because originally they were under the ocean, then rose above sea level exposing variations of rock, some with fossils, some agatized.

Hunting and identifying minerals like crystals of calcite, sapphires, agates, and iron ore furnishes an exciting opportunity for a family outing. The rocks encase fossilized species representing the earliest history of Montana and Wyoming. .

Yellowstone River agate

Petrified wood occurs when the wood fiber is replaced by silicates to look as though it happened yesterday.

Fort Union

Fort Union was built by the American Fur Company in 1828 near the confluence of the Yellowstone and Missouri Rivers. The fort was the great trading place of the Missouri and Yellowstone Country and much more than a military outpost. Fort Union was the New York City of the west. Among its famous visitors were George Catlin, Emperor Maximilian, and John Audobon.

Indians, Americans, French, and English traded peacefully here. During the best years, 110,000 beaver, deer, buffalo, and other skins were shipped downriver to St. Louis.

The riverboat, Yellowstone, round-tripped continuously between St. Louis and Fort Union keeping approximately one hundred employees busy swapping with the Indians and trappers. Few coins changed hands; the bartered goods were guns, tobacco, beads, blankets, and tools.

Fort Union was the Timbuktu of North America. Adventurers visited the Missouri-Yellowstone country outpost in order to earn bragging rights over a drink in Philadelphia, Boston, or New York.

After the fur trade era, the fort was abandoned and dismantled, but from the early blueprints, the Department of the Interior rebuilt the fort in 1987. It is located eleven miles north of Fairview, Montana across the Missouri River.

Today the fort averages about thirty thousand visitors a year who find an abundance of historic signs posted expressing the old memories.

Now we have come full circle. We began with Lewis and Clark's first visit to Montana, then looked at the mountains, studied the history and geology, and explored the human activities along the Yellowstone River. We hope you're enticed to come.

The fort commander lived in a magnificent home while other fort personnel dwelt in rather miserable surroundings.

The temperate northern desert is fragile. Plants barely survive the low rainfall, hot summers, and cold, dry winters. Overgrazing by wild game herds is a problem; their numbers need to be held in check.

Even though care must be taken, the desert is a special area. Its face is exposed. Rocks and landscapes are easy to view but fragile. Desert recreation includes hiking and four-wheeling, and seeing the numerous species of birds and animals.

It is important to understand how careful we must be.

A place for squirrels to gather nuts should be interwoven with the master plan for his future as well as ours...

The old fur trappers could find solitude -
We still have some -
But will these places be here tomorrow?

If you decide to come here to live, remember living together carries responsibility.

Conclusion

We are finishing a century like no other in man's history. We have passed from free range to barbed-wire, from the horse to the jet plane to the rocket; we have walked on the moon and floated through space.

We expanded our minds with computers but continue to work arithmetic problems by adding zeros.

We embraced free love and found AIDS. Now we are searching for the family values of the homesteader who lived on the cold, Montana plain.

During the process of change, the population pressure and visitors on Montana and Wyoming's Yellowstone Country will be incomprehensible. We must have fewer children and recycle our waste in order not to be buried in our own muck.

Think...how many times a trout on the Big Horn River will need to be caught and released to give an outdoor experience to future fly fishermen. Think...how many "spotted owl" episodes will threaten the economy and cause unrest. Think...how many snow-making machines will be needed for future skiers.

The number of golfers has grown thirty-fold since Eisenhower's days at Augusta National.

The social order is making adjustments but progress is slow and painful. So, people who desire to hold onto the past will need to squeeze harder, while people living in the future will need to plan for better utilization. As the economy heads into the future, it must grow slowly and steadily, providing for real employment.

The world will need better use of plastics and their recycling. Fifty years from now antiques will be wood or metal objects such as brass lamps. Do not throw away these real earth things because of their increasing value.

What's ahead? Maybe, Mars, Jupiter and further while here at home we will have to learn how to live in better harmony closer together.

Your children will demand all that life promises and they will not take no for an answer.

Glossary

Archean: oldest rock; formed before most life on earth

Basalt: dark stone from a volcanic flow; often hardened into columns

Bentonite: clay formed from collected volcanic ash and usually sodium from a shallow sea

Caldera: the area or depression inside an inactive volcano

Chinook: Indian name for the warm, winter wind descending the mountains

Chugwater: soft, red rock formation of the Triassic time

Climate zones: temperature and rainfall variations

Compression: shifting continental plates placing pressure on other plates

Continental plates: large blocks of rock surface of land areas

Cretaceous: see Earth Age Chart

Crustaceans: see Earth Age Chart

Desert: area of scant vegetation and rainfall

Devonian: period of time; see Earth Age Chart

Eocene: see Earth Age Chart

Fossil: remains of a prehistoric creature

Glacier: large ice field

Gneiss: metamorphic rock with coarse grains, sometimes banded; can expose minerals of quartz and feldspar

Granite: intrusive igneous rock often pink in color

Jurassic: see Earth Age Chart

Laramide orogeny: time of mountain-building episodes during which the Rocky Mountains were created

Limestone: rock formed from sediment having an abundance of skeletons of sea creatures

Mesozoic: see Earth Age Chart

Metamorphic rock: rock created from heat and pressure deep within the earth

Miocene: see Earth Age Chart

Mountain fault: where seperation in rock surfaces occur usually up or down

Ordovician: see Earth Age Chart

Paleocene: see Earth Age Chart

Palladium: metal used in industry

Plate stacking: compression pushing sedimentary stratas positions from horizontal to vertical

Platinum: precious metal used in industry

Pre-Cambrian: see Earth Age Chart

Rhyolite: reddish stone from a volcanic flow

Sandstone: soft rock of pressed sand

Sedimentary strata: layer of rock from sediment

Tertiary: see Earth Age Chart

Travertine: limestone rock from minerals of a hot spring

Triassic: see Earth Age Chart

Uplift: the movement of a continental plate during compression

Volcano: a fracture in the Earth's mantel allowing molten rock to flow out onto the surface

Bibliography

Abarr, Don. 1989. *Hoofbeats on the Wind.* Columbus, MT: The Stillwater Sun.

Alstad, Ken. 1994. *Savvy Sayin's.* Tucson, AZ: Ken Alstad Company.

Abarr, Don. 1989. *Hoofbeats on the Wind.* Columbus, MT: The Stillwater Sun.

Alstad, Ken. 1994. *Savvy Sayin's.* Tucson, AZ: Ken Alstad Company.

Alt, David D. and Donald W. Hyndman. 1972. *Roadside Geology of the Northern Rockies.* Missoula, MT: Mountain Press Publishing.

Anderson, Bob. 1994. *Beartooth Country Montana's Absaroka and Beartoth Mountains.* Helena, MT: Montana Magazine.

Baldwin, Ewart M. 1964. *Geology of Oregon.* Eugene, OR: University of Oregon Cooperative Bookstore.

Bramlett, Jim. 1992. *Ride for the High Points: The Real Story of Will James.* Missoula, MT: Mountain Press Publishing Company.

British Museum. 1985. *Dinosaurs and Their Living Relatives.* London and Cambridge, Great Britain: British Museum and Press Syndics of Cambridge University.

Brown, Bruce and Lane Morgan. 1990. *The Miracle Planet.* New York: Gallery Books.

Bureau of Business and Economic Research. *Twenty-first annual Economic Outlook Seminar.* University of Montana, Missoula. January, 1996.

Dannen, Kent and Donna Dannen. 1981. *Rocky Mountain Wildflowers.* Estes Park, CO: Tundra Publications.

Department of Natural Resources and Conservation for the State of Montana. *Montana Oil and Gas Annual Review.* Vol. 38. August, 1995.

Dippie, Brian W. 1982. *Remington & Russell.* Austin, TX: University of Texas Press.

Dippie, Brian W. "Government Patronage: Catlin, Stanley, and Eastman." *Montana,* Vol. 44, No. 4 (Autumn, 1994): 40-53.

Ewing, Sherm. 1995. *The Ranch: A Modern History of the North American Cattle Industry.* Missoula, MT: Mountain Press Publishing.

Feldman, Robert. 1985. *The Rockhound's Guide to Montana.* Helena, MT: Falcon Press.

Fritz, William J. 1985. *Roadside Geology of the Yellowstone Country.* Missoula, MT: Mountain Press Publishing.

Gordon, Albie, Margaret Lehfeldt, and Mary Morsanny. 1971. *Dawn in Golden Valley.* Visalia, CA: American Yearbook Company.

Gordon, Paul. 1990. *Bighorn Canyon National Recreation Area.* Helena, MT: Falcon Press.

Graves, F. Lee. 1994. *Montana's Fur Trade Era.* Helena, MT: American and World Geographic Publishing.

Hager, Mark. 1970. *Fossils of Wyoming.* Laramie, WY: University of Wyoming.

Harris, Burton. 1993. *John Colter.* Lincoln, NB: University of Nebraska Press.

Henckel, Mark. 1985. *The Hunter's Guide to Montana.* Helena, MT: Falcon Press.

Jensen, Earl R. 1987. *Flowers of Wyoming's Big Horn Mountains and Big Horn Basin.* Basin, WY: Basin Republican Rustler Printing.

Lagerson, David R. and Darwin R. Spearing. 1988. *Roadside Geology of Wyoming.* Missoula, MT: Mountain Press Publishing.

McDowell, Bart. "CM Russell Cowboy Artist." *National Geographic,* Vol. 169, No. 1 (January, 1986): 46-50.

McPhee, John. 1988. *Outcroppings.* Salt Lake City, UT: Peregrine Smith Books.

McRae, W.C. and Judy Jewell. 1994. *Montana Handbook.* Chico, CA: Moon Publications.

Meloy, Mark. 1986. *The Mountain Ranges of Eastern Montana Islands on the Prairie.* Helena, MT: Montana Magazine.

Montana Magazine. 1992. *My Montana.* Helena, MT: Montana Magazine, American and World Geographic Publishing.

O'Brien, Mary Barmeyer. 1995. *Bright Star in the Big Sky.* Helena, MT: Falcon Press.

O'Hara, Pat. 1991. *Wilderness Scenario Peaceful Images of the Wind.* Helena, MT: American & World Geographic Publishing.

Pellant, Chris. 1990. *Rocks, Minerals, and Fossils of the World.* Boston: Little, Brown and Company.

Peterson, Harold. 1969. *The Last of the Mountain Men.* Cambridge, ID: Backeddy Books.

Rattenbury, Richard C. 1993. *Packing Iron: Gunleather of the West.* Millwood, NY: Zon International Publishing Company.

Reese, Rick. 1991. *Greater Yellowstone the National Park and Adjacent Wildlands.* Helena, MT: Montana Magazine.

Rhodes, Frank H.T., Herbert S. Zim, and Paul R. Shaffer. 1962. *Fossils.* New York: Golden Press.

Roundup, Montana, Museum Historical Research Committee, comp. 1974. *Roundup on the Musselshell.* Roundup, MT: The Roundup Record-Tribune.

Russell, Osborne. Aubrey L. Haines and Norma Tirrell, eds. 1955. *Rocks, Minerals, and Fishes of the World.* Lincoln, NB: University of Nebraska Press.

Sandoz, Mari. 1966. *The Battle of the Little Big Horn.* Lincoln, NB: University of Nebraska Press.

Schneider, Bill. 1985. *Montana's Yellowstone River.* Helena, MT: Montana Magazine.

Shirley, Gayle C. 1993. *Four-legged Legends of Montana.* Helena, MT: Falcon Press.

Stegner, Wallace. 1954. *Beyond The Hundredth Meridian.* New York: Penguin Books.

Stone, Robert. 1994. *Day Hikes in the Beartooths.* Red Lodge, MT: Yellowstone Printing.

Thomas, Phillip Drennon. "Slice of Heart: Holiday Greetings from Charles M. Russell." *Southwest Art,* Vol. 24, No. 7 (December, 1994): 46-50.

Thomas, David Hurst, Jay Miller, Richard White, Peter Nabokov, and Philip J. Deloria. 1993. *The Native Americans: An Illustrated History.* Atlanta, GA: Turner Publishing, Inc.

Thompson, Ida. 1982. *National Audubon Society Field Guide to North American Fossils.* New York: Alfred A. Knopf.

Tirrell, Norma. 1995. *Montana.* Oakland, CA: Compass American Guides.

Van West, Carroll. 1986. *A Traveler's Companion to Montana History.* Helena, MT: Montana Historical Society Press.

Vestal, Stanley. 1946. *Jim Bridger Mountain Man.* Lincoln, NB: University of Nebraska Press.

Vestal, Stanley. 1952. *Joe Meek The Merry Mountain Man.* Lincoln, NB: University of Nebraska Press.

White, Richard S. and Robert E. Short, eds. 1988. *Achieving Efficient Use of Rangeland Resources: Papers Presented at the Fort Keogh Research Symposium.* Bozeman, MT: Montana State University Agricultural Experiment Station.

Wilkinson, Todd. 1991. *Greater Yellowstone National Forests.* Helena, MT: Falcon Press.

Zim, Herbert S. and Hurst J. Shoemaker. 1987. *Fishes.* New York: Golden Press.

Consultants
Henry E. Reed, Geologist
Gary Leppart, Geologist
Jay Spielman, Geologist
George Long, Historian

Introduction of the Author
and
Synopsis of the Book

Tom Thayer lived in Oregon from 1941 until 1981 when he moved to Montana and lived on a cattle ranch for several years before moving to Billings to continue in the business of insurance and agricultural financial planning.

During life in Oregon, Tom attended Western Oregon College of Education playing on the schools first undefeated football team and completed his master's degree from the University of Oregon in 1954.

After coaching and teaching in the Oregon school systems for eleven years his amateur photography hobby became his occupation. He worked with CBS News for the next 14 years. During this time, Tom's work took him to cover the Alaskan earthquake, Viet Nam, Kruschev's Canadian trip, and many political stories with Rockefeller, Robert Kennedy, Nixon, McGovern, and others. During this time his scope was broadened with travel and discussion with commentators like Charles Kuralt, Bill Kurtis, Dan Rather, Bill Plante, Ike Pappas, and others.

Now retirement time has rolled around and he has time to expand some of his creative ideas. The book "The Yellowstone River Country of Montana and Wyoming" is a photo-journal covering the topics of early Indians, fur traders, an and trappers, settlements and is interspersed with the geology and geography. The geology covers the formation of the Rocky Mountains and how this happening created the present climate. The geology also is responsible for the natural resources of timber, metals, oil, and recreation. The book looks at the Big Horn Mountains, Pryor Mountains, and the mountain areas of the Absaroka and Beartooths. The formation of Yellowstone Park is illustrated with volcanic drawings and photographs although the discussion shows more how this affected the surrounding geography. It then flows into the present activities starting with small towns in Wyoming to Montana and illustrates the economic activities as the river flows to the Missouri in Williston, North Dakota. Montana is visited by 8 million people annually and Yellowstone Park captures another 3.1 million.

From the standpoint of reading and viewing material of this area there seems to be an unquenchable demand. The feeling is most books deal with a single topic showing more of the beauty and not how we live with the mountains, rivers, and countryside, the theme of which may easily be "We live with the environment."